Sharing Secrets

The Mount Sinai Hospital Auxiliary wishes to express its appreciation to our corporate sponsors who have so graciously donated to this project.

Sharing
Secrets

Edited by
Rona Cappell and Elise Mecklinger

A fundraising project of the
Mount Sinai Hospital Auxiliary

MOUNT
SINAI
HOSPITAL

National Library of Canada Cataloguing in Publication Data

Main entry under title:
    Sharing secrets

Includes index.
ISBN 0-9689679-0-6

    1. Cookery, Jewish. I. Cappell, Rona, 1958-
II. Mecklinger, Elise III. Mount Sinai Hospital Auxiliary (Toronto, Ont.)

TX7147.S4459 2001   641.5'676   C2001-903514-4

Edited by Rona Cappell and Elise Mecklinger

    2   3   4   5   05   04   03   02

Book design by Counterpunch/Peter Ross
Printed and bound in Canada by Transcontinental Printing

This book can be purchased in bulk for corporate gift giving.
For details contact:
Mount Sinai Hospital Auxilliary,
600 University Avenue, room 208,
Toronto, Ontario
M5G 1X5.
Telephone: 416-586-8290.
Fax: 416-586-5239.
Toll free: 1-888-509-8290.
Email: auxiliary@mtsinai.on.ca.
Or reach us visit our web site at www.mtsinai.on.ca.

Table of Contents

Acknowledgments

It is our pleasure to present to you *Sharing Secrets*. This is not the first time that our friendship has led us down a creative and philanthropic path. As Co-Chairman of the Mount Sinai Hospital Auxiliary's *Perspectives* magazine, 1999, we were able to contribute to the Auxiliary's "Breathe Life Into Birth Campaign." Now with *Sharing Secrets* we are privileged to offer another important fundraising initiative.

There are many people who must be thanked for their participation in this most worthwhile charitable endeavour:

Firstly, a thank-you to our corporate sponsors — Kellogg's, Parmalat, Unico, Italpasta, Unilever, Quaker and SERCA. We thank you for your generosity and your support.

We greatly acknowledge the skilled contributions of Peter Ross and Linda Gustafson, our energetic and creative design team from Counterpunch.

Our eight-page pictorial could not have been possible without the kindness and advice of Tony Moniz of D&G Graphics and Pusateri's Fine Foods.

Special thanks to Norene Gilletz of Gourmania Inc. for sharing her wisdom and expertise with us throughout this project. Her input was superb and invaluable.

Thanks to our copy editor Wendy Thomas, and Lori Rennie of Transcontinental Printing.

As always, thanks to photographer Hudson Taylor, of Taylor and Associates, for his long-standing support of our organization.

Thanks also to Fran McBride and David Davenport of the Public Relations Department of The Mount Sinai Hospital.

Many thanks to Heather Reisman for her support of this project.

Special thanks to Joe Mapa, President and CEO of Mount Sinai Hospital, who has continued to be a source of encouragement for this proud endeavour.

Special thanks to our dear friends Auxiliary President Marlene Borins and Past President Hinda Silber for their encouragement and moral support. Thanks also to our Executive Director Cindy Berk and her staff for their input and expertise.

And finally to those special men in our lives — the Cappell men, Rob, Max and Eric, and the Mecklinger men, Alan, Shawn, Jordy and Dave — for your wisdom and unconditional support.

We proudly present to you the fruits of our labour.

Rona & Elise.

Whetting Your Appetite

Hot Artichoke and Spinach Dip

Yield: 2 cups.

> 1 14-oz. can artichokes, drained and chopped
> 1 cup mayonnaise
> 1 cup shredded Mozzarella cheese
> ⅛ tsp. garlic powder
> 1 10-oz. package frozen spinach, thawed and drained

1. Place ingredients in a large ovenproof casserole and mix thoroughly with a wooden spoon. Bake uncovered in preheated 350 degree oven for 25 minutes, until hot and bubbly.

2. Transfer to a serving bowl. Serve immediately with crackers or crudités.

By Barbara Bregman

Baked Artichoke Dip

Pour this scrumptious hot dip into a hollowed-out round bread. Cut the bread you've removed into bite-sized cubes to serve with the dip.

Yield: 2 cups.

> 1 14-oz. can artichokes, drained
> ½ cup grated Parmesan cheese
> 1 cup regular mayonnaise (not light)
> ½ tsp. garlic salt
> Dash of lemon juice

1. Place artichokes in the work bowl of a food processor. Pulse until finely chopped, about 10 seconds. Add the rest of the ingredients and process another 10 to 15 seconds, until well blended.

2. Transfer to a small ovenproof casserole dish and bake uncovered in preheated 350 degree oven for 10 to 15 minutes, until piping hot.

By Harriette Laing

Herbed Garlic Dip with Pita Chips

Yield: 2 cups.

DIP
½ lb. (250 g) cream cheese, cut in chunks
1 cup plain yogurt
1 tsp. minced fresh garlic
1 tsp. minced fresh thyme leaves

Place all ingredients in the work bowl of a food processor and process until well mixed. Chill before serving.

PITA CHIPS
3 or 4 pitas
¼ cup olive oil
½ tsp. minced fresh garlic

1 With scissors, cut each pita into quarters. In a small bowl, whisk together olive oil and garlic.

2 Place the pita pieces on baking sheets. Using a pastry brush, brush the pita pieces with oil mixture.

3 Bake in preheated 475 degree oven for 5 minutes, or until lightly browned.

By Queenie Nayman

Hot Feta and Tomato Spread

Yield: 4 servings.

1 cup crumbled feta cheese
2 plum tomatoes, thinly sliced
2 tbsp. olive oil
2 tbsp. chopped fresh oregano
Freshly ground black pepper

Serve this tasty spread with pita and black olives.

1 Spread feta cheese evenly on the bottom of a sprayed 2-cup ovenproof baking dish.

2 Arrange tomato slices in an overlapping fashion over the cheese. Drizzle oil over the tomatoes. Sprinkle with oregano and pepper.

3 Broil 2 to 3 inches from heat until cheese is bubbling, about 5 to 8 minutes.

By Marla Hertzman

Sun-Dried Tomato Pesto on Brie

This easy appetizer is great for company.

Yield: 6 to 8 servings.

¼ cup sun-dried tomatoes, coarsely chopped
1 cup boiling water
2 tsp. olive oil
2 tsp. minced fresh garlic
2 tsp. balsamic vinegar
½ tsp. dried basil
¼ cup chopped fresh parsley
Salt and pepper to taste
2 packages (each 125 g) round Brie cheeses, or 1 larger sized Brie

1 Place tomatoes in a mixing bowl. Pour boiling water over tomatoes and let stand for 15 minutes. Drain well.

2 In a small skillet, heat oil over medium heat. Add sun-dried tomatoes, garlic, vinegar and basil to skillet. Cook for 1 minute. Remove from heat and stir in parsley. Season with salt and pepper to taste. Let cool.

3 Cut rind off the top of each cheese. Place on a baking sheet that has been sprayed with cooking spray. Top with tomato mixture. (Can be prepared to this point, covered and refrigerated for up to 1 day.)

4 Bake uncovered in preheated 350 degree oven for 5 to 10 minutes, or until cheese melts slightly.

By Pearl Weiss

NOTES:

Cranberry Cheese

Yield: 8 servings.

¾ cup goat cheese
½ cup plain yogurt
1½ tbsp. honey
1½ cups fresh cranberries
1 tbsp. sherry or port
⅛ tsp. cinnamon
Pinch ground ginger

Serve this delicious dip with sliced fruit such as apples, pears or chunks of pineapple.

1 Place goat cheese, yogurt and honey in the work bowl of a food processor. Process about 10 seconds, until well blended. Transfer to a mixing bowl.

2 Process cranberries, sherry, cinnamon and ginger until smooth, about 20 seconds. Stir the cranberry purée into the cheese mixture and mix thoroughly.

By Queenie Nayman

Tuna Tarts

Yield: 8 tarts.

1 7-oz. can flaked white tuna, drained
1 cup shredded Mozzarella cheese
⅓ cup green pepper, finely chopped
¼ cup Miracle Whip salad dressing
1 8-oz. can refrigerated crescent rolls

1 In a mixing bowl combine tuna, cheese, green pepper and salad dressing.

2 Separate dough into 8 triangles. Press into ungreased muffin tins to form tart shells. Divide tuna mixture evenly among tart shells.

3 Bake in preheated 375 degree oven for 12 to 15 minutes, until golden.

By Toni Baille

Dumplings in Red Pepper Sauce

Yield: 6 servings.

RED PEPPER SAUCE
1 tsp. olive oil
1 medium onion, finely chopped
2 tsp. minced fresh garlic
½ tsp. chili powder
1 19-oz. can plum tomatoes, undrained
3 medium red peppers, cut in ½-inch dice
1 tbsp. sugar
1 tbsp. balsamic vinegar
¼ cup chopped fresh parsley
1 tbsp. minced fresh basil
2 tbsp. freshly grated Parmesan cheese

1 In a large saucepan, heat oil over medium heat. Sauté onion and garlic for 2 to 3 minutes, or until softened. Sprinkle with chili powder.

2 Add tomatoes, red peppers, sugar and vinegar. Bring to a boil and then reduce heat to low. Cover and simmer for 30 to 40 minutes, or until peppers are soft. Add parsley, basil and cheese; simmer for another 10 minutes.

3 Place sauce in the work bowl of a food processor and process for about 20 seconds, or until thoroughly blended. (The sauce can be prepared up to a day in advance and stored in the refrigerator. It can either be served hot or at room temperature.)

FILLING
2 tsp. olive oil
1 bunch green onions, thinly sliced, green parts removed
½ tsp. minced fresh garlic
¼ cup thinly sliced button mushrooms
¼ cup pine nuts
1 cup partly skimmed ricotta cheese
¼ cup freshly grated Parmesan cheese
2 egg whites
1 tbsp. minced fresh basil

1 In a large saucepan, heat oil over medium heat. Add green onions, garlic, mushrooms and pine nuts. Sauté for 2 to 3 minutes, or until mushrooms and onions are softened. Place in a large mixing bowl.

2   Add ricotta and Parmesan cheeses, egg whites and basil to the bowl. Blend mixture thoroughly with a fork.

> DUMPLINGS
> 1 tsp. cornstarch
> ¼ cup cold water
> 18 wonton wrappers
> Additional cornstarch to dust work surface and cookie sheet

1   Dissolve cornstarch in water; set aside.

2   Slightly dampen each wonton wrapper by sprinkling it with a few drops of water. Place diagonally on a work surface that has been dusted with cornstarch.

3   Place a heaping teaspoon of filling in the middle of each wrapper.

4   Fold in half, joining bottom point with top point.

5   Dip thumb and index finger into cornstarch mixture. Seal edges, being sure to make an airtight seal. Repeat until all the wrappers are used. Place dumplings on a cookie sheet that has been dusted with cornstarch. (Dumplings can be assembled, covered and refrigerated for 2 to 3 hours.)

6   In a large skillet, bring 2 inches of water to a simmer over medium heat. With a slotted spoon, carefully lower dumplings in batches into the water. Simmer for about 5 minutes, or until dumplings appear soft.

7   Pour 1 cup Red Pepper Sauce onto a deep serving platter. Arrange dumplings on top.

By Elise Mecklinger

NOTES:

Smoked Trout Mousse

Serve this tasty spread with crackers, crudités or pita chips. For a pretty presentation, pipe it into hollowed-out cherry tomatoes.

Yield: 3 cups.

2 cups smoked trout fillet (about 1 lb. fillets, skinned and flaked)
1 bunch green onions, thinly sliced, using 2 inches of the green part
⅓ cup chopped celery
½ cup mayonnaise
½ cup cream cheese
1 tsp. minced fresh garlic
1 tbsp. minced fresh parsley
¼ tsp. salt
¼ tsp. pepper

1 Place all ingredients in the work bowl of a food processor. Process with on/off turns, until mixture is blended but still chunky.

2 Spoon into a decorative bowl. Refrigerate 4 hours or overnight.

By Elaine James

Cheddar Pennies

The dough can be prepared in advance, shaped into rolls and refrigerated or frozen until needed. Perfect for unexpected guests!

Yield: about 6 dozen.

1 lb. old Cheddar cheese, grated
½ cup butter, softened
1¼ cups flour

1 Place all ingredients in a large bowl and knead by hand until evenly blended. Take small batches and place in work bowl of a food processor. Process for a few seconds, until thoroughly blended. Briefly knead batches of dough together by hand.

2 Shape dough into 2 logs, each 1½ inches in diameter. Wrap in plastic wrap and refrigerate for several hours, until cold enough to slice into ¼-inch slices.

3 Place ½ inch apart on parchment-lined baking sheets. Bake in preheated 350 degree oven for 10 to 12 minutes.

By Queenie Nayman

Garlic Parmesan Crisps

Yield: 2 dozen.

½ cup oil
2 tsp. minced fresh garlic
1 tsp. dried oregano
1 tsp. paprika
2 tbsp. grated Parmesan cheese
1 8-oz. can Pillsbury refrigerated crescent rolls
1 tbsp. sesame seeds

1 In a small bowl, whisk together oil, garlic, oregano, paprika and cheese. Let stand 3 hours.

2 Separate dough into 8 triangles. Cut each triangle into thirds lengthwise. Twist each piece of dough to form a twisted shape.

3 Place on a cookie sheet that has been lightly sprayed with cooking spray. Sprinkle twists with sesame seeds.

4 Bake in preheated 400 degree oven for about 10 minutes, or until golden brown.

5 Put twists in a bowl and toss with marinade.

By Trudy Cappell

NOTES:

Imitation Crab Crostini

Crostini are small rounds of toasted bread topped with patés or dips. This delicious crab mixture makes a terrific crostini topping or can be spooned into endive spears.

Yield: about 2 dozen.

BASIC CROSTINI

1 8-oz. baguette (at least 12 inches long), cut diagonally into ½-inch slices

2 tbsp. olive oil

1 Place baguette slices on a cookie sheet. With a pastry brush, spread olive oil over top.

2 Bake uncovered in preheated 400 degree oven until slices are golden and crispy, about 6 to 8 minutes. Alternatively, grill each side on the barbecue for about 2 minutes.

3 Cool the crostini, cover and store for up to 1 day in an airtight container.

IMITATION CRAB APPETIZER

1 lb. imitation crabmeat

½ each red, yellow and orange peppers, cut in ¼-inch dice

1 bunch green onions, thinly sliced, green parts removed

4 tbsp. ultra low-fat Miracle Whip salad dressing

Juice of ½ a small lemon

1 tbsp. chopped fresh dill

½ − 1 tsp. pepper

1 Place crabmeat, peppers and onions in a large mixing bowl. Mix together with a spoon.

2 Add salad dressing and lemon juice and stir until well mixed. Sprinkle with dill and pepper and mix again. (Can be prepared up to a day in advance and refrigerated.)

3 Spread on crostini.

By Rona Cappell

Gravlax

Yield: 30 to 40 servings.

4 to 4½ lbs. centre-cut fresh salmon, halved lengthwise, entirely boned, skin on
1 large bunch of dill, washed and dried
2 tbsp. cracked white pepper
½ cup sugar
⅓ cup coarse pickling salt

1 Use tweezers to remove any small pin bones from salmon. Place one half, skin side down, in a large glass baking dish or casserole. Arrange the entire bunch of dill evenly over salmon.

2 In a small bowl, combine pepper, sugar and salt. Sprinkle evenly over dill. Place the other piece of salmon on top, skin side up.

3 Cover dish with foil. Place a platter on top of foil, then place heavy weights or cans on the platter to weigh down the salmon. Place in the refrigerator.

4 Marinate for 3 days. Turn fish over every 12 hours and baste with its juices.

5 To slice, remove from casserole and scrape away dill and spices. Place each fillet skin side down on a carving board. Slice salmon diagonally into paper-thin slices, detaching each slice from the skin.

6 Serve chilled with Mustard Dill Sauce and thin slices of buttered black bread.

MUSTARD DILL SAUCE
4 tbsp. spicy mustard
1 tsp. dry mustard
3 tbsp. brown sugar
2 tbsp. white vinegar
⅓ cup vegetable oil
3 tbsp. chopped fresh dill

In a small bowl, mix together the mustards, brown sugar and vinegar until well blended. Add the oil in small spoonfuls, blending after each addition with a wire whisk until mixture reaches a mayonnaise-like consistency. Stir in chopped dill.

By Elaine James

This easy company dish is an excellent alternative to smoked salmon!

Potato Pancakes with Smoked Salmon Topping

These easy potato pancakes can be prepared in advance, then reheated in a preheated 400 degree oven for 8 to 10 minutes, until crispy and hot.

Yield: about 2 dozen.

POTATO PANCAKES
2½ lbs. (about 4 large) baking potatoes, peeled and cut in quarters
1 medium onion, peeled and cut in quarters
3 large eggs, slightly beaten
1 tsp. salt
⅛ tsp. pepper
¼ cup matzo meal (or 2 to 3 tbsp. flour)
¼ cup oil for frying

TOPPING
1 cup sour cream or plain yogurt
1 tbsp. minced fresh dill
2 bunches green onions, thinly sliced, green parts removed
1 8-oz. package smoked salmon

1 Fit food processor with the shredding disc. Shred the potatoes and onion. Place shredded mixture on paper towels and squeeze out the excess moisture. Place in a large mixing bowl.

2 Add eggs, salt, pepper and matzo meal and combine thoroughly with a spoon. Let stand for 5 minutes.

3 In a large skillet, heat oil over medium heat. Drop potato mixture by tablespoons into the hot oil. Brown on each side until golden, about 2 to 3 minutes, turning once. Drain well on paper towels.

4 In a small mixing bowl, whisk together sour cream, dill and green onions.

5 To serve, top pancakes with strips of smoked salmon and top with a dollop of sour cream mixture.

By Elaine James

Chicken Fricassee

Yield: 12 servings as an appetizer or 8 servings as a main dish.

2 tbsp. olive oil

2 large onions, finely chopped

2 stalks celery, thinly sliced

2 cups tomato juice

2 cups water

1 package (200 g) chicken gizzards, quartered

1 lb. chicken necks, cut in 1-inch pieces

2 lbs. lean ground beef

1 tsp. garlic powder

1 tsp. onion powder

½ tsp. Worcestershire sauce

12 chicken wings, halved

Salt and pepper to taste

1 tbsp. cornstarch

2 tbsp. water

As a variation to this traditional dish, add 5 or 6 cut-up chicken livers and ½ lb. sautéed mushrooms.

1 In a large soup pot, heat oil over medium heat. Add onions and sauté until translucent, about 4 to 5 minutes. Add celery and cook 2 minutes longer. Add tomato juice and water and bring to a boil.

2 Reduce heat to low and add gizzards and necks. Cover and simmer for ½ hour.

3 In a large mixing bowl, mix together ground beef, garlic powder, onion powder and Worcestershire sauce. Form mixture into small balls and add to simmering sauce.

4 Cook for 20 minutes, then add chicken wings and cook ½ hour longer. Season with salt and pepper.

5 In a small bowl, whisk together cornstarch and water. Stir into sauce and continue to cook another 2 minutes, until thickened. Serve over plain white rice or mushroom fried rice.

By Ruth Frisch

Goat Cheese and Pesto Tortilla Pizzas

Yield: 8 servings.

PESTO
1½ cups fresh basil, stems removed
½ cup fresh parsley, stems removed
½ cup freshly grated Parmesan cheese
½ cup vegetable broth or low-fat chicken broth
¼ cup fresh bread crumbs
¼ cup pine nuts
2 tbsp. minced fresh garlic
¼ cup olive oil

Place basil, parsley, cheese, broth, crumbs, nuts and garlic in the work bowl of a food processor. Process for 30 seconds. While the machine is running, add oil and process for another 30 seconds, or until well blended.

PIZZAS
8 flour tortillas (6 inches in diameter)
2 tbsp. olive oil
1 tsp. minced fresh garlic
1 small purple onion, cut in ¼-inch dice
1 cup sliced mushrooms
¼ cup sun-dried tomatoes (oil-packed), finely chopped
1 recipe Pesto (above)
1 cup shredded skim milk Mozzarella cheese
½ cup goat cheese, crumbled

1   Place tortillas on a cookie sheet that has been sprayed with cooking spray. Bake in preheated 350 degree oven for 5 minutes. Set aside.

2   In a large skillet, heat oil over medium heat. Sauté garlic, onion, mushrooms and sun-dried tomatoes for 2 to 3 minutes.

3   Spread equal amounts of pesto on the surface of each tortilla. Top with equal amounts of vegetable mixture. Sprinkle with Mozzarella cheese; top with goat cheese.

4   Bake in preheated 400 degree oven for 8 minutes, until piping hot.

By Elise Mecklinger

Rainbow Crystal Fold

Yield: about 2 dozen.

These flavour bundles wrapped in lettuce leaves make a wonderful appetizer.

4 cups water
½ lb. vermicelli noodles, broken in pieces
1 tbsp. oil
1 tsp. minced fresh ginger
1 tsp. minced fresh garlic
1½ to 2 lbs. mixture of ground chicken and beef
2 medium carrots, thinly sliced
2 stalks celery, thinly sliced
½ cup water chestnuts
2 tbsp. cooking sherry
2 tbsp. soy sauce
1 tsp. sesame oil
¼ cup hoisin sauce
1 or 2 heads of iceberg lettuce, washed, dried and separated into individual leaves

1 In a large saucepan, bring water to a boil. Add vermicelli and boil until tender, about 7 minutes. Drain, rinse under cold water and set aside.

2 In a large skillet, heat oil over medium heat. Add ginger and garlic and sauté 1 minute. Add meat mixture and sauté until cooked, about 7 minutes, stirring occasionally. Add carrots, celery and water chestnuts; cook about 2 minutes longer. Remove from heat.

3 In a small bowl, whisk together sherry, soy sauce and sesame oil. Pour over meat mixture, add vermicelli and mix well with a wooden spoon.

4 Take a lettuce leaf, brush the inside with hoisin sauce and spoon 1 to 2 tbsp. meat mixture on top. Roll up lettuce leaf to make a packet. Repeat with remaining lettuce, hoisin sauce and meat mixture.

By Hinda Silber

Asparagus Moo Shu with Mushrooms

In order to eat one of these gracefully, fold up the bottom and hold tight!

Yield: 6 servings.

12 small flour tortillas
3 tbsp. rice wine (sake) or dry sherry
2 tbsp. soy sauce
1 tbsp. sesame oil
1 tsp. cornstarch
¼ tsp. black pepper
2 tbsp. canola oil, divided
3 eggs, beaten
1 tbsp. minced fresh ginger
1 tbsp. minced fresh garlic
1 bunch thin asparagus, cut diagonally into 2-inch pieces
2 bunches green onions, thinly sliced, using 2 inches of the green part
½ cup mushrooms, thinly sliced, stems removed
1 cup hoisin sauce

1 Stack tortillas and wrap in tinfoil. Bake in preheated 325 degree oven for 20 minutes.

2 Meanwhile, in a small bowl, whisk together rice wine, soy sauce, sesame oil, cornstarch and pepper. Set aside.

3 In a large skillet or wok, heat 1 tbsp. of the oil over medium heat. Add eggs and scramble lightly. Remove to a plate and set aside.

4 Add remaining oil to pan and heat over medium heat. Add ginger and garlic and sauté for 3 minutes. Add asparagus, onions and mushrooms and sauté 2 to 3 minutes longer.

5 Add rice wine mixture and eggs to the skillet. As soon as the sauce thickens, transfer ingredients to a serving platter.

6 Remove tortillas from the oven. With a pastry brush, spread each tortilla with hoisin sauce. Divide asparagus mixture evenly among tortillas. Roll into cylinders.

By Rona Cappell

Chicken Satays

Yield: 4 to 5 dozen.

¼ cup peanut butter

3 tbsp. soy sauce

3 tbsp. lime juice

1 tbsp. brown sugar

1 tsp. minced fresh garlic

½ tsp. hot pepper sauce

6 boneless, skinless single chicken breasts, cut lengthwise in 1-inch strips

1 To make peanut sauce, combine first 6 ingredients in a mixing bowl and mix until thoroughly blended.

2 Place chicken strips in a glass baking dish. Pour sauce over chicken and mix to coat evenly. Cover and refrigerate at least 2 hours or overnight.

3 Preheat the barbecue. Thread chicken onto skewers. Place skewers on the hot barbecue and grill 4 to 5 minutes per side, until cooked through. (Alternatively, these can be broiled in the oven.) Discard any remaining marinade. Serve immediately.

By Esther Mecklinger

NOTES:

This Indonesian favourite consists of bite-sized pieces of meat or poultry threaded on skewers, served with a spicy peanut sauce. Soak wooden skewers in cold water for about ½ hour to prevent them from burning.

Sushi Pizza

The Japanese call this dish Oshi-Zushi or pressed sushi. It really should be prepared in a wooden box or "oshi waku," but a 9-inch springform pan is a good substitute. It can be cut up and served just like pizza!

Yield: 10 to 12 servings.

SUSHI RICE

2 cups short or medium-grain uncooked rice

2 cups + 2 tbsp. water

4 tbsp. rice vinegar

2 tbsp. + 1 tsp. sugar

1 tsp. salt

1 Place the rice in a colander and rinse thoroughly. Let drain for ½ hour.

2 Place rice and water in a heavy saucepan with a tight-fitting lid. Bring to a boil over medium-high heat. Reduce heat to low; let simmer, covered, for 15 minutes.

3 Remove saucepan from heat. Remove the lid, stretch a clean tea towel over the pan and replace the cover. Let stand for 15 minutes to finish steaming.

4 In a small saucepan, heat rice vinegar, sugar and salt over medium heat. Whisk until sugar dissolves. Set aside and let cool.

5 Put the hot rice into a bowl. Drizzle vinegar mixture over the rice and mix it by cutting into the rice with a wooden spatula or spoon, then folding it. Repeat this cutting and folding process until the liquid is thoroughly blended.

6 Do not refrigerate. Keep the rice covered with a clean towel at room temperature for no longer than an hour.

TO ASSEMBLE

6 to 8 slices thinly sliced cucumber

1 carrot, peeled and cut into matchsticks

2 cups imitation crab pieces

3 tbsp. rice vinegar

1½ tbsp. sugar

¼ tsp. salt

Pickled ginger slices, to garnish

1 Coat a 9-inch springform pan with cooking spray. Fill with half of the sushi rice. Arrange cucumber slices on top of rice, then add the carrots. Place the remainder of the sushi rice over top.

2 Place imitation crab in a medium mixing bowl. In a small bowl, whisk together vinegar, sugar and salt. Pour over crab.

3   Arrange crab mixture on top of the second rice layer. Cover with plastic wrap. Place a
     weight on top of the plastic and leave it on for 15 minutes.

4   Remove sides from springform pan; cut into wedges or smaller pieces. Serve with pickled
     ginger. Leftovers can be refrigerated for up to a day.

    By Elise Mecklinger

Spiced Mixed Nuts

Yield: 3 cups.

You can prepare these nuts a week in advance. Store them in an airtight container.

    2 egg whites, slightly beaten
    2 cups dry roasted peanuts
    ½ cup whole almonds
    ½ cup walnut halves
    ¾ cup sugar
    1 tbsp. pumpkin pie spice (or ½ tbsp. nutmeg, 1 tsp. cinnamon and ½ tsp. cloves)
    ¾ tsp. salt

1   In a medium bowl, combine egg whites with peanuts, almonds and walnuts. Stir until
     well coated.

2   In a small bowl, whisk together sugar, spice and salt. Add to nuts and mix well.

3   Spread nuts in a single layer on a cookie sheet that has been sprayed with cooking spray.
     Bake in preheated 300 degree oven for 20 to 25 minutes, until medium brown, stirring
     occasionally. Remove and cool on wax paper. Break up into large clusters.

    By Esther Mecklinger

Empanada

This Tex-Mex classic resembles the Italian calzone. Place it on a serving platter, cut it in wedges and serve it as a first course.

Yield: 6 servings.

FILLING
1 tbsp. olive oil
2 tsp. minced fresh garlic
1 medium onion, finely chopped
2 small potatoes, peeled and cut in 1/2-inch dice
2 medium carrots, thinly sliced
1 lb. lean ground chicken
½ cup fresh green peas
Salt and pepper to taste

1 In a large skillet, heat oil over medium heat. Add garlic, onion, potatoes and carrots; sauté for 2 minutes. Stir in ground chicken and peas. Reduce heat to medium low. Cover to allow meat and vegetables to cook, about 10 minutes, stirring occasionally.

2 Remove cover. Season with salt and pepper. Drain off any excess liquid. Allow filling to cool.

CRUST
1½ cups flour
1 tsp. salt
1 tbsp. sugar
½ cup butter or margarine
⅓ cup water
Additional water to brush edge of dough

1 Place flour, salt and sugar in a large mixing bowl. Whisk together until thoroughly blended. Add the butter or margarine; cut in with a pastry blender until mixture is crumbly. Sprinkle water over mixture. Using a spoon, form into a ball of dough. Wrap well and refrigerate for 1 hour.

2 Roll dough out on a lightly floured surface into a large circle about ¼ inch thick. Place filling in the centre, leaving a 1-inch border exposed around the outer edge of the circle.

3 Using a pastry brush, moisten exposed edge of dough with water. Fold in half, forming a half moon. Seal the edges well with a fork. Carefully transfer to a lightly greased baking sheet.

4 Bake in preheated 350 degree oven for 20 to 30 minutes, until golden.

By Cora Hahn

Stirring the Pot

Blender Gazpacho

Serve this summer-time favourite with chopped green onions, croutons and a dollop of sour cream or yogurt.

Yield: 4 servings.

1 cup peeled and chopped tomatoes
½ cup finely chopped green peppers
½ cup finely chopped celery
½ cup peeled, finely chopped cucumber
¼ cup finely chopped green onions
2 tsp. minced fresh garlic
2 tbsp. minced fresh parsley
2 cups tomato juice
2½ tbsp. red wine vinegar
2 tbsp. olive oil
½ tsp. Worcestershire sauce
1 tsp. salt
¼ tsp. freshly ground pepper

1 Place tomatoes, peppers, celery, cucumber, green onions, garlic and parsley in a blender and purée for about 30 seconds.

2 Add remaining ingredients and purée 20 seconds longer.

3 Pour soup into a jar or large mixing bowl and refrigerate until ready to serve.

By Annette Addison

NOTES:

Spicy Squash Soup

Yield: 8 to 10 servings.

1 tbsp. butter or margarine

4 leeks (white part and 1 inch of green part), quartered lengthwise and thinly sliced

2 medium carrots, thinly sliced

4 cups acorn or butternut squash, peeled and cut in 2-inch chunks

½ tsp. allspice

½ tsp. nutmeg

1 tsp. ground cinnamon

1 tsp. dried thyme (or to taste)

½ to 1 tsp. red pepper flakes (depending on how hot you like it)

8 cups vegetable broth

1 In a large soup pot, heat butter over medium heat. Sauté leeks for 1 to 2 minutes. Add carrots and squash. Sauté for 3 to 5 minutes, until veggies are soft. (If veggies start to burn, add a little broth.)

2 Add allspice, nutmeg, cinnamon, thyme and red pepper flakes and sauté another 2 minutes.

3 Add broth and bring to a boil. Reduce heat to simmer, cover and cook for 20 minutes, until tender.

4 In a food processor or blender, process soup in batches for 15 seconds, or until puréed. (Alternatively, use an immersion blender and purée soup right in the pot.)

By Candy Schnier

Ladle soup into pretty serving bowls and garnish with a dollop of sour cream or plain yogurt and chopped chives.

Spiced Tomato Bisque

The fish base for this easy bisque is provided by clamato juice. If desired, substitute tomato juice and a dash of Worcestershire sauce.

Yield: 4 to 6 servings.

3 tbsp. butter or margarine
¼ cup onion, chopped
1 medium carrot, peeled and grated
½ English cucumber, peeled and chopped
½ tsp. minced fresh basil
1 28-oz. can tomatoes
¼ cup celery tops, finely chopped
1 to 2 cups clamato juice
Salt and pepper to taste
½ to 1 oz. gin or vodka

1   In a large skillet, heat butter or margarine over medium heat. Add onion, carrot, cucumber and basil, then sauté for 3 to 5 minutes, until soft.

2   Place veggie mixture, tomatoes and celery in a blender and purée until almost smooth. Stir in clamato juice until desired consistency is reached. Season with salt and pepper. Chill before serving.

3   To serve, drizzle a little liquor into each of the serving bowls. Add tomato bisque and stir.

By Judy Freedman

NOTES:

_____

_____

_____

_____

_____

_____

_____

_____

_____

_____

_____

_____

_____

_____

_____

Broccoli and Cauliflower Soup

Yield: 6 servings.

2 tbsp. olive oil

1 medium onion, finely chopped

2 carrots, thinly sliced

1 bunch broccoli, broken into florets

1 medium cauliflower, broken into florets

4 cups water

4 tsp. instant chicken soup mix

¼ tsp. pepper

1 tbsp. fresh dill

Salt to taste

Garnish this easy soup with finely chopped parsley, dill or chives.

1 In a large saucepan, heat oil over medium heat. Add onion and sauté for 2 to 3 minutes, until translucent. Add carrots, broccoli and cauliflower and sauté another 2 minutes.

2 Add water and soup mix and bring to a boil. Reduce heat to low, add pepper and fresh dill, cover and simmer until veggies are tender, about 8 minutes.

3 Purée soup in batches in a blender or a food processor until smooth. Add salt if needed.

By Esterita Rajsky

Cauliflower and Potato Soup

Yield: 6 servings.

6 medium potatoes, cut in chunks

½ medium cauliflower, broken into florets

2 leeks, coarsely chopped

2 tbsp. instant chicken soup mix

Water to cover

Salt and pepper to taste

Purée this simple soup to the consistency you like. It's best when it is slightly chunky rather than completely smooth.

Place all ingredients in a large soup pot. Bring to a boil over high heat. Reduce heat to low. Cover and simmer for 45 minutes. Adjust seasonings to taste. Purée until desired texture is reached.

By Hinda Silber

Summer Strawberry Soup

Soups are not necessarily reserved for cold seasons. This easy, refreshing soup is sure to please family and friends.

Yield: 4 to 6 servings.

4 cups strawberries
1 cup plain yogurt
1 cup vanilla yogurt
½ cup orange juice
1 tsp. grated lemon rind
¼ cup white sugar
½ cup water
⅛ tsp. cinnamon
Sliced strawberries, to garnish

Place all ingredients in a blender or the work bowl of a food processor. Purée or process until smooth. Chill for a few hours before serving. Garnish with sliced strawberries.

By Elise Mecklinger

Best Bean Soup

Beans, barley, lentils and peas are all terrific sources of soluble fibre.

Yield: 8 servings.

½ cup red beans
½ cup white beans
3 cups water
2 tbsp. olive oil
1 medium onion, cut in ½-inch dice
1 cup sliced mushrooms
1 cup carrots, thinly sliced
1 cup celery, thinly sliced
8 cups chicken or vegetable broth (homemade or canned)
⅓ cup mixture of barley, lentils and split peas (yellow or green)
Salt and pepper to taste

1 Place red and white beans in a large saucepan. Cover with water and bring to a boil. Cook for 2 minutes. Remove from heat and let soak for 1 hour. Discard any beans that are floating. Drain and rinse well; set aside.

2 In a large saucepan, heat oil over medium heat. Sauté vegetables for 2 to 3 minutes, or until softened.

3 Add broth, drained beans and barley mixture and bring to a boil. Reduce heat to simmer. Cover and simmer for 2 hours, stirring occasionally. Season with salt and pepper.

By Eleanor Long

Chunky Lentil Soup

Yield: 8 servings.

This healthy, hearty soup is sure to please family and friends.

2 tbsp. olive oil
2 tsp. minced fresh garlic
1 medium onion, finely chopped
1 medium potato, peeled and cut in ¼-inch dice
2 carrots, sliced in ½-inch rounds
2 stalks celery, thinly sliced
1 19-oz. can plum tomatoes, with their juice
2 cups red lentils
½ tsp. dried thyme
½ tsp. dried cumin
6 cups chicken or vegetable broth
Salt and pepper to taste

1 In a large soup pot, heat oil over medium heat. Sauté garlic, onion and potato for 5 to 7 minutes. Add carrots and celery and cook another 2 to 3 minutes.

2 Add tomatoes and reduce heat to medium-low. Stir in lentils, thyme and cumin.

3 Add broth and bring to a boil, stirring often. Reduce heat to low. Cover and simmer for 35 to 40 minutes, or until lentils are soft.

4 Place half of the soup in the work bowl of a food processor. Process for 15 seconds, or until puréed. Return puréed mixture to the pot and blend with the remaining soup. Season to taste with salt and pepper.

By Rona Cappell

Chunky Mediterranean Fish Soup

You won't have to fish for compliments when you serve this tasty soup!

Yield: 8 servings.

2 tsp. olive oil
2 medium onions, finely chopped
2 tsp. minced fresh garlic
2 tbsp. water
1 28-oz. can tomatoes, undrained
4 cups chicken broth
2 cups potato, cut in ½-inch dice
1 cup carrot, thinly sliced
1 cup celery, cut in ½-inch dice
3 cups spinach, washed and torn into bite-sized pieces
1½ lbs. fresh sole fillets, cut in 1-inch cubes
1 tsp. crushed fennel seeds
Dash hot pepper sauce
Salt and pepper to taste

1   In a large soup pot, heat oil over medium heat. Add onions and garlic and sauté for 1 minute. Add water, cover and cook until onions are soft, about 3 minutes.

2   Add tomatoes and mash coarsely with a potato masher. Add chicken broth, potato, carrot and celery. Bring to a boil. Reduce heat to low. Cover and simmer for 10 minutes, or until vegetables are tender.

3   Stir in spinach, sole, fennel seeds and hot pepper sauce. Season with salt and pepper to taste. Simmer uncovered for about 10 minutes, or until fish is opaque and flakes easily with a fork. Taste and adjust seasonings if necessary.

By Carol Lavine

Southwest Corn Chowder

Yield: 6 servings.

For a lighter version, substitute light evaporated milk for the cream.

1 tsp. vegetable oil

6 cups fresh sweet corn kernels

1 large Vidalia or sweet onion, finely chopped

2 tsp. minced fresh garlic

1 jalapeno pepper, seeded, ribs removed, finely chopped

3 cups vegetable broth

2 cups light cream

Salt and pepper to taste

1 tbsp. lime juice

6 cups water

1 small potato, peeled and cut in ½-inch cubes

½ red pepper, cut in ½-inch cubes

½ orange pepper, cut in ½-inch cubes

1 tbsp. finely chopped cilantro, to garnish

1   In a large pot, heat oil on medium-low heat. Set aside ¾ cup corn kernels. Add remaining corn kernels and onion to pot. Sauté for 8 to 10 minutes, until onions are soft. Add garlic, jalapeno pepper and vegetable broth. Increase heat to medium and bring to a boil, stirring frequently. Reduce heat to low and simmer for 15 minutes.

2   Stir in cream and simmer 5 minutes longer. Remove from heat. In the work bowl of a food processor, process soup in batches until smooth, about 10 to 15 seconds. Season with salt, pepper and lime juice. Set aside and keep warm.

3   In a medium pot bring water to a boil. Add potato cubes and cook for 2 minutes. Add reserved corn kernels and cook 2 minutes longer. Add pepper cubes and cook for another 2 minutes. Drain the vegetables and add to warm corn chowder. Pour into serving bowls and garnish with cilantro.

By Debra Verk

Minestrone Soup with Mini Matzoh Balls

This scrumptious soup is an excellent example of fusion cuisine!

Yield: 8 to 12 servings of soup, about 4 dozen Matzoh balls.

¼ cup vegetable oil
2 tbsp. minced fresh garlic
1 small onion, finely chopped
1 leek (white part and 1 inch of green), quartered lengthwise and thinly sliced
2 carrots, cut into ¼-inch rounds
2 small zucchini, cut in ½-inch cubes
1 small sweet potato, cut in ½-inch cubes
7 cups chicken broth
1 28-oz. can tomatoes
¼ cup chopped fresh parsley
¼ cup chopped fresh basil
Salt and pepper to taste
Mini Matzo Balls (below)

1 In a large soup pot, heat oil over medium heat. Sauté garlic, onion, leek, carrots, zucchini and sweet potato over medium heat for 5 minutes.

2 Add broth and tomatoes and bring to a boil.

3 Reduce heat to low. Add parsley and basil. Cover and simmer for 1 to 1 ½ hours. Season with salt and pepper. Serve with matzo balls.

MINI MATZOH BALLS
2 tbsp. pareve margarine
1 bunch green onions, thinly sliced, green parts removed
4 eggs
2 tbsp. vegetable oil
1 tsp. salt
¼ tsp. pepper
1 cup matzoh meal
6 cups water or chicken broth

1 In a medium skillet, melt margarine over medium heat. Add green onions and sauté until wilted, about 2 to 3 minutes. Set aside.

2 In a large mixing bowl, whisk together eggs, oil, salt and pepper with a wire whisk. Stir in matzoh meal and onions. Cover and refrigerate until firm, about 2 hours.

3   Line a cookie sheet with a sheet of wax paper. Dip hands into cold water and roll round-ed teaspoons of matzoh ball mixture into balls. Place on cookie sheet. Chill 30 minutes.

4   In a large saucepan, bring water or broth to a boil. Slip the matzoh balls into the broth. Reduce heat to simmer. Cover and cook about 30 minutes. Remove with a slotted spoon and serve in soup.

By Elise Mecklinger

Mushroom Zucchini Soup with Tarragon and Mustard

Yield: 6 to 8 servings.

3 tbsp. olive oil
1 tbsp. minced fresh garlic
1 medium onion, cut in ¼-inch dice
1 medium zucchini, cut in ¼-inch dice
2 medium potatoes, peeled and cut in ¼-inch dice
1 cup thinly sliced button mushrooms
6 cups chicken or vegetable broth
1 tsp. dried tarragon
1 tsp. dried mustard
1 tsp. salt
Freshly ground pepper to taste

1   In a large soup pot, heat oil over medium heat. Sauté garlic, onion, zucchini, potatoes and mushrooms for 2 to 3 minutes, or until wilted and golden.

2   Add broth to soup pot and bring to a boil. Add tarragon, mustard and salt. Reduce heat to simmer and cover. Cook about 20 minutes, until vegetables are tender.

3   In food processor or blender, process soup in batches for 15 seconds, or until puréed. Return soup to pot. Season with freshly ground pepper.

By Sylvia Naftolin

Fresh Corn Chowder

Yield: 8 servings.

2 tbsp. butter
1 large onion, finely chopped
3 stalks celery, finely chopped
1 red pepper, finely chopped
4 cups raw fresh sweet corn (4 or 5 cobs)
1 tsp. salt (or to taste)
1 tsp. pepper
1 tbsp. chopped fresh thyme (or 1 tsp. dried)
1 tbsp. chopped fresh basil (or 1 tsp. dried)
7 cups vegetable broth

1   In a large soup pot, heat butter over medium heat. Add onion and sauté 2 minutes. Add celery and red pepper and cook 2 to 3 minutes longer. Add corn and seasonings and stir until well mixed.

2   Add broth and bring to a boil. Reduce heat to low. Cover and simmer for 10 minutes.

3   In the work bowl of a food processor, process soup in batches for 10 to 15 seconds, until puréed.

4   Return purée to a saucepan and heat over medium-low heat. Do not boil. Adjust seasonings to taste.

By Nonie Plener

Sweet Potato and Pepper Soup

This versatile soup may be served cold or hot. It also freezes well.

Yield: 6 to 8 servings.

¼ cup vegetable oil
1 medium onion, finely chopped
2 yellow or orange peppers, cut in ¼-inch cubes
2 to 3 tsp. curry powder (optional)
3 large sweet potatoes, peeled and cut in chunks
6 cups chicken or vegetable broth
Salt and pepper to taste

1 In a large soup pot, heat oil over medium heat. Add onion and peppers and sauté for 3 to 5 minutes, until softened. Sprinkle with curry powder and cook another 2 minutes.

2 Add sweet potatoes and broth and bring to a boil. Reduce heat to low. Cover and simmer until sweet potatoes are soft, about 30 minutes.

3 Place soup in batches in a blender or food processor and purée. Pass soup through a strainer or food mill to remove any pepper skins.

By Sandy Hausman

Chicken Soup à la Mother-in-Law Luba

Yield: 8 servings.

1 soup chicken (3½ to 4 lbs.)
Water to cover chicken (about 8 cups)
1 large onion
2 parsnips
3 carrots
3 stalks celery
½ cup lima beans
½ bunch fresh parsley
1 tbsp. salt
1 tsp. sugar
White pepper to taste

Instead of using a whole chicken, sometimes I just get chicken bones from the butcher. You'll need enough bones to fill your pot half full. If you are using a soup chicken, make the soup a day ahead so you can skim off the fat before serving.

1 Put chicken in a large soup pot and cover with water. Bring to a boil over medium-high heat. Remove the scum from the top of the soup as it appears.

2 Peel vegetables, cut them in chunks and add to soup along with remaining ingredients. Reduce heat to low. Simmer partially covered for at least 2 hours.

3 Remove the chicken and vegetables from the broth. Let soup cool slightly, then refrigerate overnight. The next day, skim the fat from the top of the soup. Reheat soup and serve. (The boiled chicken and vegetables can either be served in the soup or separately.)

By Jacquie Kolber

Old-Fashioned Chicken Soup

This recipe produces a rich and flavourful broth that is delicious on its own or can be used as a base for other soups. Serve with matzoh balls and/or noodles for a traditional Jewish starter.

Yield: 12 to 15 servings.

4 to 5 lbs. chicken pieces and/or bones
(a stewing hen is ideal)
2 or 3 pieces of beef marrow bones
Cold water
1 large onion, cut in chunks
3 or 4 large carrots, cut in chunks
2 parsnips, cut in chunks
3 or 4 stalks celery, cut in chunks
1 small turnip, cut in chunks
1 tbsp. salt (or to taste)
Whole black peppercorns
Small bunch fresh parsley
Small bunch fresh dill
1 bay leaf
Salt and pepper to taste
Additional chopped dill, to garnish

1 Place chicken pieces and/or bones and marrow bones in a large stockpot. Cover with water so that the meat is covered by 2 to 3 inches of water. Bring to a boil over high heat. Reduce heat to simmer. Remove foam and scum with a slotted spoon.

2 Add vegetables, salt and peppercorns to the soup. Simmer partially covered on low heat for 1 ½ hours.

3 Tie parsley and dill together with kitchen string. Add to soup along with bay leaf. Continue to simmer for 1 to 1 ½ hours. If necessary, add more water to keep chicken covered.

4 Let broth cool slightly. Drain through a sieve into clean containers and refrigerate for several hours or overnight. Remove congealed fat from broth and discard. (Note: To serve right away, pour broth through a gravy/fat separator.)

5 Reheat to serve. Garnish with chopped dill. If desired, serve with some of the chicken from the chicken pieces. Season with salt and pepper to taste. Refrigerate or freeze extra soup.

By Linda Waks

Bubie Elsie's Chicken Barley Soup

Yield: 8 servings.

This soup is great for the winter.

10 cups cold water
1 cup pearl barley, well rinsed
Chicken bones from 1 chicken, or 2 double
    chicken breasts with bones
3 cloves garlic
1 medium onion
4 or 5 carrots
3 stalks celery, cut in half crosswise
Salt and pepper to taste
4 to 5 cups water
4 or 5 potatoes, cut in bite-sized chunks
Salt and pepper to taste

1 Fill a large soup pot with water. Add barley, chicken, garlic, onion, carrots and celery. Add salt and pepper. Bring to a boil over high heat. Skim off all the foam and any bits that rise to the top.

2 Reduce heat to low. Simmer with the lid mostly covering the pot but open enough to allow the steam to escape.

3 After the soup has been simmering for about 1 hour, place 4 to 5 cups water in a saucepan and bring to a boil over high heat. Add potatoes. Reduce heat to medium-low and cook for about 20 minutes, until tender.

4 Using a slotted spoon, remove onion from soup and discard. Remove garlic and carrots from soup and put them on a plate. Mash them together with a fork, then put them back in the soup.

5 Using a slotted spoon, add potatoes to the soup. Continue simmering for at least another half hour. (The soup should cook 1½ to 2 hours in total.) Add salt and pepper to taste.

By Cindy Berk

Pea Soup With Dumplings

For a heartier soup, you can substitute little meatballs for the dumplings.

Yield: 8 servings.

6 pieces flanken (short ribs)
8 cups water
3 tbsp. barley
1 bunch of carrots, cut in ½-inch dice
4 stalks celery, cut in 1-inch chunks
1 parsnip, cut in ½-inch rounds
1 package Streit's pea soup mix
1½ tsp. chopped fresh dill
Salt and pepper to taste
Dumplings (below)

1 Place flanken and water in a large soup pot. Bring to a boil over high heat. Skim off any foam and any bits that rise to the top. Add the next 6 ingredients. Reduce heat to low. Partially cover with the lid and simmer for 1 to 1½ hours. Season with salt and pepper to taste.

2 Prepare Dumplings as directed below and drop into simmering soup. Cook 5 minutes longer.

DUMPLINGS
1½ cups flour
¼ tsp. baking powder
3 eggs, lightly beaten
1½ cups water
Salt and pepper to taste

Place all ingredients in a large mixing bowl. Stir until thoroughly combined. Drop by teaspoonfuls into the simmering soup. Dumplings will rise to the top when they are done.

By Trudy Cappell

Getting into the Skinny

Summer Fruit Salad

For an attractive presentation, layer the fruit in a glass bowl instead of mixing it together.

Yield: 6 servings.

HONEY ORANGE DRESSING
⅓ cup orange juice
2 tbsp. lemon juice
1½ tbsp. honey
¼ tsp. dried ginger

Whisk together ingredients in a mixing bowl.

FRUIT SALAD

1 large mango, peeled and cut in ½-inch cubes
2 cups blueberries
2 cups green seedless grapes
2 bananas, sliced in ½-inch rounds
1 cup strawberries, halved
2 peaches or nectarines, unpeeled and thinly sliced
1 recipe Honey Orange Dressing (above)

Arrange fruit in layers in a large glass bowl. Drizzle the dressing over the fruit. Chill before serving.

By Shari Borenstein

NOTES:

Spinach Salad with Strawberries or Mandarin Oranges

Yield: 4 to 6 servings.

SESAME POPPY SEED DRESSING

¼ cup cider vinegar

¼ to ½ cup sugar (to taste)

2 tbsp. sesame seeds

1 tbsp. poppy seeds

2 tsp. finely chopped onion

¼ tsp. Worcestershire sauce

¼ tsp. paprika

½ cup vegetable oil

Place first 7 ingredients in the work bowl of a food processor. Process for 10 seconds, until blended. Add oil through the feed tube and blend another 10 seconds. (Can be prepared a day or two in advance and refrigerated.)

SALAD

1 lb. fresh spinach, torn into bite-sized pieces
    (or mesclun salad greens, romaine or a combination)

2 cups fresh strawberries, halved and hulled
    (or mandarin oranges, fresh or canned)

½ cup slivered toasted almond

Sesame Poppy Seed Dressing (above)

Place spinach, strawberries and almonds in a large salad bowl. At serving time, toss with dressing.

By Faith White

Strawberry Pecan Spinach Salad

Use any other sweet berries or slivered almonds if you prefer.

Yield: 4 to 6 servings.

RASPBERRY DRESSING

¼ cup sugar (or 2 packets artificial sweetener)

1½ tbsp. poppy seeds

¼ tsp. paprika

¼ cup raspberry vinegar

2 tsp. onion, finely chopped

½ tsp. Worcestershire sauce

½ cup vegetable oil

Place all ingredients in a container with a tight-fitting lid. Shake well to blend. Shake again before using. (Can be prepared in advance and refrigerated.)

SWEET PECANS

2 tbsp. water

¼ cup sugar

½ cup pecans, coarsely chopped

1   In a large nonstick skillet, combine water, sugar and pecans. Heat over medium-low heat about 5 minutes, stirring constantly. The sugar will melt to a golden brown and coat the pecans.

2   Pour onto a square of greased foil or parchment paper. When cool, break into small pieces.

SALAD

1 lb. spinach, torn into bite-sized pieces

2 cups strawberries, sliced

1 recipe Raspberry Dressing (above)

1 recipe Sweet Pecans (above)

Place spinach and strawberries in a large salad bowl. At serving time, drizzle with dressing and toss. Sprinkle sweet pecans over top and lightly toss again.

By Harriet Bomza

Field Salad with Red Peppers, Blackened Pecans and Balsamic Vinaigrette

Yield: 6 to 8 servings.

BALSAMIC VINAIGRETTE
3 tbsp. balsamic vinegar
1 tsp. minced fresh garlic
1 tbsp. Dijon mustard (or use half Dijon, half grainy mustard)
1 cup olive oil
Salt and pepper to taste

Whisk together first 3 ingredients in a mixing bowl. Gradually drizzle in the oil and whisk until blended. Add salt and pepper.

SALAD
1 head Boston lettuce
1 head radicchio
1 bunch arugula
1 Belgium endive
½ red pepper, thinly sliced
2 tbsp. vegetable oil
¼ cup pecan halves
1 recipe Balsamic Vinaigrette (above)

1   Wash and dry salad greens. Tear into bite-sized pieces. Arrange salad greens and red pepper decoratively on a large serving platter.

2   In a small skillet, heat oil over medium heat. Add pecans and sauté for 2 to 3 minutes, or until they begin to brown. Flip them over and sauté 2 to 3 minutes on the other side. Remove with a slotted spoon and drain well on paper towels.

3   At serving time, scatter pecans over salad, then drizzle with Vinaigrette.

By Debra Verk

Watercress and Endive Salad with Orange Vinaigrette

Yield: 4 to 6 servings.

ORANGE VINAIGRETTE

¼ cup white wine vinegar

⅓ cup orange juice

½ tsp. dry mustard

1 tsp. dried tarragon

⅔ cup olive oil

Salt and pepper to taste

Whisk together first 4 ingredients in a mixing bowl. Gradually add oil and whisk until well blended.

SALAD

3 cups watercress, large stems removed

3 cups curly endive

½ cucumber, thinly sliced

1 tomato, cut in ½-inch cubes

1 small purple onion, thinly sliced

1 recipe Orange Vinaigrette (above)

Place first 5 ingredients in a large salad bowl. At serving time, drizzle lightly with some of the Vinaigrette. Toss gently to combine. (Reserve the rest of the dressing for future use.)

By Salmina Ahmed

NOTES:

Caesar Salad

Yield: 4 to 6 servings.

CAESAR SALAD DRESSING
1 2-oz. can flat anchovy fillets, drained
1 to 2 tsp. minced fresh garlic
1½ tbsp. red wine vinegar
1½ tbsp. lemon juice
½ tsp. Worcestershire sauce
2 egg yolks
¼ tsp. pepper
1 tsp. dry mustard
6 tbsp. grated Parmesan cheese
4 tbsp. olive oil
4 tbsp. vegetable oil

Place first 9 ingredients in the work bowl of a food processor. Process until thoroughly blended, about 10 seconds. While machine is running, add oils through the feed tube and process another 10 seconds, or until blended. Refrigerate until serving time.

GARLIC CROUTONS
4 tbsp. vegetable oil
1 tsp. minced fresh garlic
3 thick slices French bread, cut in 1-inch cubes

1   In a large saucepan, heat oil over medium heat. Add garlic and sauté 1 minute. Add bread cubes and stir until coated. Place on cookie sheet that has been sprayed with cooking spray.

2   Bake in preheated 350 degree oven for 15 minutes, or until lightly browned.

SALAD
1 large head Romaine lettuce, torn into bite-sized bits
1 recipe Caesar Salad Dressing (above)
1 recipe Garlic Croutons (above)

Place lettuce in a large salad bowl. At serving time, toss lettuce with salad dressing. Add croutons and toss again.

By Honey Sherman

Salad Niçoise

Yield: 8 servings.

Niçoise Vinaigrette

¼ cup white wine vinegar

½ tsp. dry mustard

1 cup olive oil

2 shallots, finely chopped

1 tsp. minced fresh garlic

2 tbsp. minced fresh parsley

1 tsp. dried tarragon

½ tsp. salt

¼ tsp. pepper

1 tbsp. capers (optional)

In a large mixing bowl, whisk together vinegar and mustard. Gradually add the oil in a thin stream. Add the rest of the ingredients and mix well.

Salad

1½ lbs. mixed baby greens

1 recipe Niçoise Vinaigrette (above)

½ lb. green beans, trimmed and steamed

½ lb. yellow beans, trimmed and steamed

1 red pepper, cut into matchsticks

1 yellow pepper, cut into matchsticks

1 lb. tiny red potatoes, cooked and peeled

2 6-oz. cans tuna, drained and broken into chunks

3 medium tomatoes, cut in quarters

3 hard-cooked eggs, quartered

6 anchovies, patted dry

¾ cup pitted Niçoise olives

Place baby greens in a large mixing bowl. Toss with about ⅓ of the dressing. Transfer to a large oval platter. Place beans, peppers and potatoes in a large mixing bowl and toss with ⅓ of the dressing. Place the tuna chunks in the middle of the greens. Arrange the beans, peppers and potatoes around the tuna. Surround with tomato and egg quarters. Arrange the anchovy fillets attractively on top. Scatter the olives over the salad. Drizzle a little of the remaining vinaigrette over top. (Any leftover dressing can be reserved for future use.)

By Elise Mecklinger

Alexander Salad

Yield: 6 to 8 servings.

Alexander Dressing
½ small onion
2 tsp. minced fresh garlic
¼ cup + 1 tbsp. lemon juice
2½ tbsp. tarragon vinegar
1 tsp. minced fresh tarragon
2 tbsp. sugar
1 tsp. salt
¼ tsp. pepper
½ tsp. dry mustard
½ cup vegetable oil

1 Place onion and garlic in the work bowl of a food processor. Process for 10 seconds, until minced. Add the next 7 ingredients and blend another 10 seconds.

2 With the processor running, add oil through the feed tube and process another 10 seconds, until well blended.

Salad
1 avocado, peeled and cut in ½-inch cubes
1 6-oz. jar artichoke hearts, drained and cut in halves
1 head Romaine lettuce, torn into bite-sized pieces
1 head Boston lettuce, torn into bite-sized pieces
1 small radicchio, separated into individual leaves
¼ English cucumber, thinly sliced
½ red pepper, thinly sliced
1 pint cherry or grape tomatoes
1 recipe Alexander Dressing (above)

Place all vegetables in a large mixing bowl and toss until combined. Add salad dressing and toss until thoroughly mixed.

By Debra Verk

Dartmouth Salad

During World War II, my husband Morry and I lived in Dartmouth, Nova Scotia, where he was stationed in coastal artillery. As a very young bride, I found the kitchen a formidable place. Luckily, my landlady took pity on me and taught me how to cook. This is one of her recipes. Morry and I have been married 56 years. This recipe is 56 years young!

Yield: 6 to 8 servings.

DARTMOUTH SALAD DRESSING
1 medium onion, finely chopped
2 tsp. minced fresh garlic
½ tsp. salt
1 tsp. paprika
2 tsp. dry mustard
¼ tsp. pepper
¼ to ½ cup sugar (to taste)
1 cup white vinegar
1 10-oz. can tomato soup, undiluted
1 tsp. Worcestershire sauce
1 cup oil

Place all ingredients in a large jar and shake vigorously. Alternatively place the first 10 ingredients in the work bowl of a food processor and process for 10 seconds. With the machine running, pour the oil through the feed tube and process another 10 seconds, until thoroughly blended.

SALAD
12 cups torn mixed salad greens, or any variation of greens and veggies
1 recipe Dartmouth Salad Dressing (above)

Wash and dry salad greens. Place in a large salad bowl. At serving time, add salad dressing and toss until combined.

By Ida Clarfield

Unique Salad

Yield: 6 servings.

UNIQUE DRESSING

2 tsp. cider vinegar

1 tsp. lemon juice

2 tbsp. soy sauce

⅓ cup sugar

¾ cup sunflower seeds

½ cup oil

Whisk together first 5 ingredients until blended. Gradually add oil and whisk until well blended.

SALAD

1 to 2 tbsp. butter

¾ cup slivered almonds

2 3-oz. packages ramen noodles, broken up

1 head bok choy, thinly sliced

1 bunch green onions, thinly sliced

1 recipe Unique Dressing (above)

1   In a large saucepan, melt butter over medium heat. Add almonds and sauté for 2 minutes. Add noodles and sauté another few minutes. Set aside.

2   Place bok choy and green onions in a large salad bowl. Add noodles. Toss with salad dressing.

By Estelle Zaldin

Snow Pea and Mango Salad

Add thinly sliced purple onion or finely chopped cilantro to this colourful salad, if desired.

Yield: 6 to 8 servings.

LEMON-LIME VINAIGRETTE
3 tbsp. lime or lemon juice
½ tsp. salt
½ tsp. pepper
½ cup vegetable oil

Whisk together the first ingredients in a mixing a bowl. Gradually add the oil and whisk until well blended.

SALAD

1 lb. snow peas, blanched
2 mangoes, peeled and thinly sliced
½ cup red pepper, finely chopped
1 recipe Lemon/Lime Vinaigrette (above)

Place snow peas, mangoes and red pepper in a salad bowl. Drizzle dressing over top. Toss gently to combine all ingredients.

By Judy Barkin

Cole Slaw

Yield: 6 to 8 servings.

½ cup sugar
¾ cup vinegar
2 tsp. salt
1 cup lemon juice
½ cup oil
1 small cabbage (about 2 lbs.), shredded
1 green pepper, finely chopped
5 carrots, shredded

In a mixing bowl, whisk together first 5 ingredients. Place cabbage, pepper and carrots in a large salad bowl. Add dressing and mix thoroughly. Chill before serving.

By Hinda Silber

Oriental Salad

Yield: 4 to 6 servings.

ORIENTAL SALAD DRESSING

¾ cup orange juice

½ cup soy sauce

½ cup rice vinegar

¼ cup sesame oil

5 tbsp. honey mustard

2 tsp. minced fresh garlic

In a mixing bowl, whisk together all ingredients for salad dressing.

SALAD

1 head Boston lettuce, torn into bite-sized pieces

½ small purple onion, thinly sliced

1 cup snow peas, cut in half crosswise

¼ cup pine nuts

1 10-oz. can mandarin oranges, drained

1 recipe Oriental Dressing (above)

Place first 5 ingredients in a large salad bowl. Toss gently with salad dressing.

By Simone Bronfman

NOTES:

Baby Beet and Orange Salad

To ensure freshness, buy beets with the greens still attached. The beet greens can be cooked just like spinach. When peeling beets, wear rubber gloves to avoid staining your hands.

Yield: 6 servings.

1½ lbs. baby beets
4 to 6 cups water
Juice of 1 orange
1 tbsp. honey
2 tbsp. sherry wine vinegar
¼ cup olive oil
6 navel oranges
Chopped fresh parsley or chervil, to garnish

1   Scrub beets. Cut off the green tops, leaving 1 inch of stem on the beets. In a large saucepan bring water to a boil. Add beets. Reduce heat to low and simmer beets until just tender, about 15 minutes. Cool and peel. Slice into ¼-inch slices. Place in a large mixing bowl.

2   In a small mixing bowl whisk together orange juice, honey and vinegar. Slowly add oil until thoroughly blended. Pour over beets and refrigerate overnight.

3   Peel the oranges, then slice horizontally into ¼-inch rounds. Drain the beets. On a large platter, alternate the beet and orange slices so they overlap each other slightly. Form rows or a winding circle. Garnish with parsley or chervil.

By Debra Verk

Carol's Corn Salad

The dressing will keep for weeks in the refrigerator. It is also delicious over mixed greens.

Yield: 4 to 6 servings.

CAROL'S SALAD DRESSING
2 cups olive oil
1 cup white vinegar
4 tsp. salt
1 tsp. pepper
2 or 3 packets sugar substitute (e.g., Sweet and Low)
4 tbsp. light mayonnaise
3 tsp. minced fresh garlic

Place all ingredients in a food processor or a blender and mix until well blended.

2 11-oz. cans corn niblets, drained
1 cup red pepper, thinly sliced
1 cup green pepper, thinly sliced
1 bunch green onions, thinly sliced, green parts removed
3 tbsp. Carol's Salad Dressing (above)

Place first 4 ingredients in a salad bowl. Add salad dressing and stir until thoroughly mixed.

By Carol Lavine

Caprese Salad

Yield: 4 to 6 servings.

6 vine-ripened tomatoes, cut in ¼-inch slices
6 pieces bocconcini cheese, cut in ¼ inch slices
5 or 6 fresh basil leaves, thinly sliced
2 tbsp. olive oil
2 tbsp. balsamic vinegar
Salt and pepper to taste
Kalamata olives, to garnish

Bocconcini are small balls of fresh Mozzarella cheese packed in water or whey.

1 Arrange tomato slices in a single layer on a large platter. Place 1 slice of cheese in between each tomato slice.

2 Sprinkle basil over tomatoes and cheese. Drizzle with olive oil and vinegar. Sprinkle with salt and pepper. Garnish platter with Kalamata olives.

By Rona Cappell

Greek Pasta Salad

Yield: 4 to 6 servings.

GREEK SALAD DRESSING

½ cup fat-free mayonnaise

½ cup fat-free plain yogurt

2 tbsp. lemon juice

1 tsp. minced fresh garlic

2 tbsp. dried oregano

½ tsp. salt

½ tsp. pepper

Whisk all ingredients together in a bowl. (Dressing can be prepared in advance and refrigerated.)

SALAD

4 cups salted water

1 lb. fusilli or rotini (spiral pasta)

1 red pepper, cut in ½-inch cubes

1 green pepper, cut in ½-inch cubes

½ cup niçoise olives

1 cup English cucumber, cut in ½-inch cubes

¾ cup crumbled feta cheese

1 recipe Greek Salad Dressing (above)

1   In a large saucepan, bring salted water to a boil. Add the pasta and boil until tender, about 7 minutes. Drain pasta, rinse under cold water and place in a large mixing bowl.

2   Add peppers, olives and cucumber to pasta and mix well to combine. Sprinkle with feta cheese. Add salad dressing and mix thoroughly with a wooden spoon. Serve chilled.

By Carol Seidman

Pasta Salad with Smoked Turkey and Tomato Basil Dressing

Yield: 4 to 6 servings.

TOMATO BASIL DRESSING

2 cups tomatoes, seeded, cored and cut in ¼-inch cubes

1 bunch green onions, thinly sliced, green parts removed

¾ cup chopped fresh basil

4 tbsp. lemon juice

2 tsp. minced fresh garlic

1 tsp. sugar

1 tsp. salt

1 tsp. pepper

4 tbsp. olive oil

In a large bowl, combine tomatoes, onions and basil. In a medium bowl, whisk together lemon juice, garlic, sugar, salt and pepper. Gradually add oil and whisk until blended.

SALAD

1 lb. pasta (e.g., penne, farfalle, rotini) cooked, rinsed and drained

2 cups smoked turkey, diced

1 cup pitted black olives, cut in half

1 recipe Tomato Basil Dressing (above)

Place cooked pasta, turkey and olives in a large salad bowl. Drizzle with salad dressing and stir until well mixed.

By Marlene Borins

Brown Rice, Tomato and Basil Salad

Yield: 4 to 6 servings.

2 cups water
1 cup brown rice
1 tsp. salt
2 tbsp. white wine vinegar
2¼ tsp. sugar
2 tbsp. olive oil
1 lb. tomatoes, cut in ½-inch cubes
1 cup green peas, steamed
½ cup chopped fresh basil
Salt and pepper to taste

1 In a large saucepan, bring water to a boil. Add rice and salt and cover. Reduce heat to low and simmer until water is absorbed and rice is tender, about 30 minutes. Transfer to serving bowl and let cool.

2 Whisk together vinegar and sugar in a small bowl. Gradually add oil and whisk until blended. Pour over rice.

3 Add tomatoes, peas and basil to rice and mix thoroughly with a wooden spoon. Sprinkle with salt and pepper.

By Rona Cappell

Orzo Salad with Feta, Olives and Peppers

Yield: 4 to 6 servings.

Orzo Salad Dressing
4 tbsp. fresh lemon juice
1 tbsp. white wine vinegar
2 tsp. fresh minced garlic
1 tsp. Dijon mustard
1¼ tsp. dried oregano
1 tsp. dried cumin
½ cup olive oil

Whisk together first 6 ingredients in a mixing bowl. Gradually whisk in oil until blended.

4 cups water
1 lb. orzo (rice-shaped pasta)
1 cup crumbled feta cheese
¼ small purple onion, finely chopped
1 cup red pepper, finely chopped
¼ cup yellow pepper, finely chopped
½ cup pitted Kalamata olives
2 tbsp. capers, drained
1 recipe Orzo Salad Dressing (above)

1   In a large saucepan bring water to a boil. Add orzo and boil until tender, about
5 to 7 minutes. Rinse and drain well. Transfer to a large salad bowl.

2   Add feta cheese, onion, peppers, olives and capers. Add salad dressing and mix
thoroughly.

By Rona Cappell

Potato Salad

Yield: 10 to 12 servings.

5 lbs. potatoes, peeled, boiled and cut in large chunks
6 hard-cooked eggs
1 bunch green onions, thinly sliced
1 red pepper, cut in ½-inch cubes
4 stalks celery, thinly sliced
½ cup chopped fresh parsley
½ to ¾ cup light mayonnaise
Salt and pepper to taste

1   Place potato chunks in a large mixing bowl. Chop 4 of the eggs, reserving the remaining
2 eggs as a garnish. Add chopped eggs to the bowl. Add green onions, red pepper, celery
and parsley and stir with a wooden spoon until mixed.

2   Add mayonnaise and stir until well mixed. Add salt and pepper to taste. Transfer potato
salad to a serving bowl. Slice reserved eggs and use as a garnish. Chill several hours
before serving to allow flavours to blend.

By May Cappell

Hearty Potato Salad

Add some cooked
chicken to make this
salad even heartier.
If adding chicken,
eliminate the yogurt
and double the
amount of mayon-
naise in the dressing
recipe.

Yield: 6 servings.

POTATO SALAD DRESSING
½ cup fat-free plain yogurt or sour cream
½ cup fat-free mayonnaise
¼ cup white wine or sherry vinegar
1 tbsp. lemon juice
2 tsp. minced fresh garlic
3 tsp. Dijon or grainy mustard
⅛ cup vegetable oil

Whisk together first 6 ingredients in a mixing bowl. Gradually add oil and whisk until well blended.

SALAD

1 cup broccoli florets
1 cup frozen green peas
5 medium potatoes, peeled, boiled and cubed
3 eggs, hard-cooked and coarsely chopped
1 bunch green onions, thinly sliced
2 stalks celery, thinly sliced
1 small red pepper, cut in ¼-inch cubes
¼ cup purple onion, finely chopped
2 medium carrots, cut in ¼-inch rounds
½ cup chopped fresh dill
1 recipe Potato Salad Dressing (above)
Salt and pepper to taste
½ tsp. paprika
2 tbsp. chopped fresh parsley

1   Fill a large saucepan fitted with a vegetable steamer with 2 inches of water. Bring to a boil over medium heat. Place broccoli and peas in the steamer. Cover and steam for 3 to 5 minutes, until tender. Transfer to a large mixing bowl. Let cool.

2   Add potatoes, eggs, green onions, celery, red pepper, onion, carrots and dill. Stir with a wooden spoon until mixed. Add salad dressing, salt and pepper. Stir until thoroughly combined. Sprinkle with paprika and parsley. Chill before serving.

By Esther Mecklinger

Sweet and Spicy Couscous Salad

Yield: 6 to 8 servings.

SWEET AND SPICY DRESSING

¼ cup orange juice

¼ cup lemon juice

¼ tsp. cinnamon

½ tsp. salt

⅛ tsp. cayenne pepper

½ cup dried cranberries (craisins)

Whisk together all ingredients until blended.

SALAD

3 cups water

1½ cups couscous

1 medium carrot, cut in ¼-inch rounds

1½ cups green and yellow beans, cut in ¼-inch pieces

1 small red pepper, cut in ¼-inch dice

⅛ cup purple onion, finely chopped

⅛ cup chopped fresh mint

1 recipe Sweet and Spicy Dressing (above)

1   In a medium saucepan, bring water to a boil. Stir in couscous and remove from heat. Cover and let stand until the water is absorbed, about 5 minutes. Transfer to a large bowl and fluff with a fork. Let cool.

2   Fill a large saucepan fitted with a vegetable steamer with 2 inches of water. Bring to a boil over medium heat. Place carrots, beans and red pepper in the steamer. Cover and steam for 3 minutes. Let cool.

3   Add vegetables, onion and mint to the couscous and mix with a wooden spoon. Add salad dressing and mix well. Refrigerate at least 1 hour before serving to allow flavours to blend.

By Hinda Silber

Couscous Chicken Salad

This is a quick, easy recipe that is perfect for a picnic or a cottage get-together.

Yield: 4 servings.

LEMON GARLIC DRESSING
1 tbsp. lemon juice
1 tsp. minced fresh garlic
¼ tsp. ground cumin
¼ tsp. hot pepper sauce
Pinch salt and pepper
4 tbsp. olive oil

In a small bowl, whisk together first 5 ingredients. Gradually whisk in olive oil until thoroughly blended.

SALAD

1¼ cups water or vegetable broth
1 cup couscous
2 boneless, skinless single chicken breasts, cooked and cut in ½-inch chunks
1 medium tomato, peeled, seeded and cut in ¼-inch cubes
1 small bunch green onions, thinly sliced, green parts removed
1 19-oz. can chickpeas, drained
¼ cup red pepper, cut in ¼-inch cubes
¼ cup minced fresh parsley
1 recipe Lemon Garlic Dressing (above)
Salt and pepper to taste

Combine water or broth with couscous in a large salad bowl. Let stand for 5 to 10 minutes, until liquid is absorbed. Add chicken, tomato, onions, chickpeas, red pepper and parsley. Drizzle with salad dressing and mix well. Add salt and pepper to taste. Refrigerate at least 1 hour before serving.

By Shanea Rakowski

Greek Tabbouleh Salad

Yield: 6 to 8 servings.

The flavour of this delicious salad improves with standing time, so it's best to prepare it in advance.

GREEK DRESSING
½ cup fresh lemon juice
2 tsp. minced fresh garlic
⅔ cup extra-virgin olive oil
Salt and pepper to taste

Whisk together lemon juice and garlic in a small mixing bowl. Gradually whisk in the oil until well blended. Season with salt and pepper.

SALAD
1 cup fine bulgur or cracked wheat
   (or 1 package tabbouleh mix)
2 cups hot water (approximately)
1 bunch green onions, thinly sliced,
   using 2 inches of the green part
1 pint grape or cherry tomatoes, halved
½ green pepper, cut in ¼-inch dice
½ English cucumber, cut in ½-inch dice
1 19-oz. can chickpeas, drained and rinsed
1 cup pitted black or green olives
2 small carrots, grated (optional)
1 cup chopped fresh parsley
½ cup chopped fresh mint
2 cups crumbled feta cheese
1 recipe Greek Dressing (above)

1   Place bulgur or cracked wheat in a large mixing bowl. Cover with hot water. Cover and let stand for 20 minutes. Drain well, pressing out the excess water. (If using tabbouleh mix, prepare according to package directions.)

2   Add the rest of the ingredients except the salad dressing. Stir to combine.

3   Pour salad dressing over the top and toss until thoroughly combined. Chill for several hours before serving.

By Harriet Bomza

Bean and Barley Salad (Summer Salad)

This fibre-packed salad tastes best served at room temperature. Prepare the rice and barley ahead of time so it will be easy to assemble the salad quickly.

Yield: 6 to 8 servings.

DRESSING WITH A PUNCH
¼ cup red wine vinegar
1 tsp. minced fresh garlic
1 tsp. chili powder
½ tsp. salt
¼ tsp. red pepper flakes
¼ tsp. black pepper
½ cup olive oil

In a mixing bowl, whisk together the first 6 ingredients. Gradually add the oil and whisk until well blended.

SALAD

Water for cooking barley and rice
½ cup pearl barley
½ cup long-grain rice
1 cup canned or cooked black beans, drained
1 cup canned or cooked red kidney beans, drained
1 cup canned corn niblets, drained
½ cup chopped green onions
1 small red pepper, cut in ½-inch cubes (optional)
¼ cup chopped fresh cilantro (optional)
1 recipe Dressing with a Punch (above)
Salt and pepper to taste

1 In a medium saucepan, bring 2 cups water to a boil. Stir in the barley. Reduce heat to low. Cover and simmer for 45 minutes, or until tender. Let cool.

2 In another saucepan, bring 1½ cups water to a boil. Stir in the rice. Reduce heat to low. Cover and simmer for 25 minutes, until tender. Let cool.

3 Transfer barley and rice to a large serving bowl. Add black beans, kidney beans, corn, onions, red pepper and cilantro. Mix well with a wooden spoon.

4 Pour salad dressing over salad and mix well. Season with salt and pepper.

By Barbara Bregman

Asian Sesame Chicken Salad

Yield: 4 servings.

ASIAN DRESSING

2 tsp. fresh minced ginger

2 tbsp. soy sauce

2 tbsp. rice wine vinegar

1 tbsp. sugar

2 tbsp. lime juice

2 tbsp. vegetable oil

In a mixing bowl, whisk together ingredients for dressing until thoroughly blended.

SALAD

4 boneless, skinless single chicken breasts

Salt and pepper to taste

1 cup sesame seeds

⅓ cup peanut oil

1 small head Chinese cabbage

1 10-oz. can water chestnuts, drained

1 bunch green onions, thinly sliced

1 red pepper, seeded, cored and thinly sliced

1 recipe Asian Dressing (above)

1 Sprinkle chicken with salt and pepper. Spread sesame seeds on a plate. Press chicken breasts into the seeds. Coat evenly on both sides.

2 In a large skillet, heat oil over medium heat. Sauté chicken about 5 minutes per side, or until no longer pink. Set aside and let cool.

3 Cut cabbage crosswise into strips ½ inch thick. Place in a large mixing bowl. Add water chestnuts, green onions and red pepper. Pour salad dressing over salad and toss until blended. Transfer to a large serving platter.

4 Cut chicken into thin strips and arrange attractively on top of salad.

By Rona Cappell

Warm Lamb Salad

Yield: 6 servings.

SHERRY VINAIGRETTE

1 tbsp. Dijon mustard
1 tbsp. sherry vinegar
1 tsp. chopped fresh tarragon
½ cup olive oil

Whisk together first 3 ingredients in a mixing bowl. Gradually add the oil and whisk until blended.

SALAD

2 tbsp. Dijon mustard
1 tsp. minced fresh garlic
1 lb. boned lamb, from the leg or shoulder
4 sprigs fresh thyme
Salt and pepper to taste
8 cups mesclun salad greens
1 recipe Sherry Vinaigrette (above)
6 tbsp. sun-dried tomatoes, thinly sliced

1 Mix together mustard and garlic in a small mixing bowl. Spread all over lamb. Sprinkle with thyme leaves, salt and pepper. Place lamb on a rack in a roasting pan.

2 Roast in a preheated 450 degree oven for 20 minutes, or until medium-rare. Remove from oven and let rest 15 minutes before carving.

3 Place mesclun salad greens in a large mixing bowl. Add salad dressing and toss until well mixed.

4 Arrange salad greens on 6 salad plates. Slice lamb thinly and place equal amounts on top of greens. Scatter sun-dried tomatoes on top.

By Debra Verk

Dressing Up

Portuguese Salad Dressing

Yield: ⅔ cup.

⅓ cup vinegar
1 tsp. minced fresh garlic
¼ tsp. dry mustard
1 tsp. salt
1 tsp. sugar
¼ tsp. dried oregano
¼ tsp. dried basil
⅓ cup vegetable oil

Whisk together first 7 ingredients in a mixing bowl. Gradually add oil and whisk until blended.

By Libby Shiller

Citrus Salad Dressing

This dressing is perfect drizzled over your favourite greens, orange slices, purple onions and toasted sliced almonds.

Yield: ¾ cup.

2 tbsp. rice wine vinegar
2 tbsp. vegetable oil
2 tbsp. orange juice
2 tbsp. brown sugar or honey
2 tbsp. soy sauce
2 tbsp. Dijon mustard
¼ tsp. sesame oil
4 grinds black pepper from a pepper mill

In a small bowl, whisk together all ingredients until thoroughly blended.

By Phyllis Pepper

Malco's Citrus Salad Dressing

Yield: 1¾ cups.

Serve this zesty dressing over your favourite greens.

Zest of 1 orange, finely chopped, blanched in hot water and drained
Juice of 1 orange
Juice of 1 lime
1 tbsp. honey
1 tbsp. Dijon mustard
Dash salt
¾ cup olive oil
¾ cup vegetable oil

Place first 6 ingredients in the work bowl of a food processor fitted with the steel blade. Pulse with several on/off turns. With machine running, add oils through the feed tube and process for 3 minutes or until thick.

By Liora Yakubowicz

Red Wine Vinaigrette

Yield: ⅔ cup.

2 tbsp. red wine vinegar
1 tbsp. soy sauce
1 tsp. pepper
½ cup olive oil

Whisk together first 3 ingredients in a mixing bowl. Gradually add oil and whisk until thoroughly blended.

By Queenie Nayman

Honey Mustard Dressing

Yield: 1½ cups.

½ cup honey
¼ cup cider vinegar
2 tbsp. Dijon mustard
1 tsp. lemon juice
1 small onion, cut in chunks
1 tsp. poppy seeds
½ cup canola oil

Place first 6 ingredients and ¼ cup of the oil in the work bowl of a food processor or blender. Process for 15 seconds. Pour remaining oil through the feed tube and process another 10 seconds, or until thoroughly blended.

By Eleanor Long

Poppy Seed Dressing

Serve this dressing over a mixture of salad greens such as baby spinach, mesclun or radicchio.

Yield: About 4 cups.

¼ cup onion, finely chopped
1½ cups sugar
2 tsp. salt
⅔ cup apple cider vinegar
2 cups vegetable oil
3 tbsp. poppy seeds

In a large mixing bowl, whisk together first 4 ingredients. Gradually whisk in oil until mixture thickens. Add poppy seeds and whisk until blended.

By Suzanne Shuchat

Diane B.'s Salad Dressing

Yield: 1¼ cups.

¼ cup balsamic vinegar
2 tsp. minced fresh garlic
3 tbsp. sugar
3 tbsp. Dijon mustard
¾ cup olive oil

In a small bowl, whisk together first 4 ingredients. Add oil gradually, whisking well until well blended.

By Simone Bronfman

Grandma Pearl's Salad Dressing

Yield: About 4 cups.

1 10-oz. can tomato soup
¾ cup white vinegar
1 tsp. minced fresh garlic
2 tbsp. dry mustard
1 cup sugar
2 tbsp. Worcestershire sauce
2 tbsp. salt
1 tsp. paprika
1½ cups oil

Place first 8 ingredients into the work bowl of a food processor. Process for 2 minutes. With the machine running, pour oil through the feed tube and process another 2 minutes.

By Caryl Schwartz

Cajun Rub

Kick chicken breasts, fish fillets, steaks and chops up a notch!

Yield: ⅓ cup.

3 tsp. salt
4 tsp. paprika
1 tbsp. powdered garlic
1 tbsp. pepper
2 tsp. onion powder
1½ tsp. dried thyme
1½ tsp. dried oregano
1 tsp. cayenne pepper

Blend all ingredients together with a fork. Coat food thoroughly and refrigerate until ready to use.

By Elise Mecklinger

Improved Upon BBQ Sauce

Marinate chicken breasts, chicken pieces, kabobs or burgers in this better-than-store-bought sauce.

Yield: 1 cup.

½ cup bottled barbecue sauce
1 tbsp. ketchup
1 tsp. minced fresh thyme
1 tsp. chili powder
3 tbsp. frozen apple juice concentrate, thawed
¼ cup brown sugar
¼ tsp. salt

Whisk together ingredients in a mixing bowl until blended.

By Rona Cappell

Sauce Par Elegance

Yield: About 3 cups sauce.

1 12-oz. can frozen lemonade
1 cup chili sauce
⅔ cup plum jam
½ cup currants
3 tbsp. soy sauce
1 tbsp. minced fresh ginger
2 tsp. curry powder

In a medium saucepan, bring all ingredients to a boil. Reduce heat to low. Simmer for 2 to 3 minutes, whisking occasionally to blend.

By Estelle Zaldin

This sauce makes an excellent all-purpose marinade. Your results will be delicious whether you grill, bake or sauté your chicken or meat.

Sugar-Free Mango Cranberry Sauce

Yield: About 2½ cups sauce.

1 bag cranberries (fresh or frozen)
2 ripe mangoes, peeled and cut into chunks
½ cup orange juice
Rind of ½ an orange
¾ to 1 cup sugar substitute (e.g., Sugar Twin)

1 In a large saucepan, heat cranberries, mangoes, orange juice and rind over medium heat. Cook until cranberries open up and mangoes are softened, about 5 to 10 minutes.

2 Remove the pan from the stove and add sugar substitute. Pour into a serving dish. Cover and cool in the refrigerator before serving.

By May Cappell

This sauce is delicious as an accompaniment for poultry.

Curried Fruit

This sauce freezes well. It makes a tasty accompaniment for chicken, veal and fish.

Yield: 8 to 10 servings.

1 28-oz. can peach halves, drained
1 28-oz. can pear halves, drained
1 14-oz. can apricots, drained
1 14-oz. can pineapple chunks, drained
1 10-oz. can mandarin oranges, drained
16 maraschino cherries
⅓ cup butter or margarine, melted
¾ cup brown sugar
2 tsp. curry powder
Dash of nutmeg

Place fruit in a single layer in a round deep ovenproof dish. In a small bowl, whisk together butter, brown sugar, curry and nutmeg. Spread over fruit. Bake in preheated 325 degree oven for 1 hour. Cool. Refrigerate overnight. Reheat before serving.

By Hilde Ronson

Versatile Fruit Sauce

Pour this sauce over ice cream, sorbet, yogurt, blintzes, crêpes, cheesecakes or plain cakes. The sky's the limit!

Yield: About 3 cups sauce.

2 lbs. (about 4 to 5 cups) strawberries, raspberries, blueberries,
    peach slices, or a combination
1 cup sugar
3 tbsp. lemon juice
¼ tsp. vanilla
2 tbsp. liqueur (Fraise, Framboise, Crème de Cassis or Peach Schnapps)

1   Place fruit, sugar and lemon juice in a medium saucepan. Mash fruit with the back of a spoon. Bring to a boil over medium heat. Reduce heat to low. Simmer for 15 minutes, mashing the berries again if necessary.

2   Transfer mixture to a blender or the work bowl of a food processor. Process for about 10 seconds, until puréed. Add vanilla and liqueur and process 2 to 3 seconds longer. When cool, refrigerate until ready to use.

By Elise Mecklinger

Black and White Bean Salsa

Yield: About 6 cups.

2 tbsp. olive oil

2 cups uncooked corn kernels, cut off the cob

1 14-oz. can black beans, drained

1 14-oz. can Great Northern white beans, drained

1 medium red pepper, cut in ½-inch cubes

2 medium tomatoes, seeded, cored and cut in ½-inch cubes

½ cup purple onion, finely chopped

2 tbsp. minced seeded jalapeno pepper

¼ cup fresh lime juice

¼ cup chopped fresh parsley

2 tsp. minced fresh garlic

1 tsp. dried oregano

1 tsp. chili powder

1½ tsp. ground cumin

½ cup olive oil

3 tbsp. freshly grated Parmesan cheese

There are several different ways to serve this versatile salsa! You can serve it in a large bowl as an appetizer with pita chips. You can also use it to stuff 8 hollowed-out tomatoes as a lunch dish or side dish. It also makes an excellent accompaniment for chicken or fish.

1   In a large skillet, heat oil over medium heat. Add corn and sauté until golden, about 3 minutes. Transfer to a large mixing bowl.

2   Add beans, red pepper, tomatoes, onion and jalapeno pepper to mixing bowl and mix thoroughly.

3   Place lime juice, parsley, garlic, oregano, chili power and cumin in the work bowl of a food processor. Blend for 10 seconds. With machine running, pour in oil and blend another 10 seconds.

4   Pour salad dressing over corn mixture and mix thoroughly. Sprinkle with Parmesan cheese.

By Marlene Borins

Sidebars

Artichoke Casserole

Yield: 8 servings.

2 tsp. olive oil
1 medium onion, finely chopped
1 tsp. minced fresh garlic
1 14-oz. can artichokes, drained and chopped (reserve liquid)
¼ cup bread crumbs
1 cup grated old Cheddar cheese
2 tbsp. chopped fresh parsley
Dash hot sauce
Pinch each of salt, pepper and dried basil

1   In a small saucepan, heat oil over medium heat. Sauté onion and garlic for 3 to 5 minutes, or until softened. Place in a large mixing bowl.

2   Add half of the reserved liquid from the artichokes to the onions. Blend thoroughly. Add artichokes along with remaining ingredients and stir until blended.

3   Place in a 7 x 11-inch baking dish that has been sprayed with cooking spray. Bake in pre-heated 325 degree oven for 30 minutes, until golden.

By Honey Sherman

Broccoli à la Rocky

Yield: 9 servings.

3 eggs, lightly beaten
½ cup mayonnaise (regular or fat-free)
½ cup Coffee Rich, water or vegetable stock
½ cup flour
3 10-oz. packages frozen broccoli, thawed and drained
½ package onion soup mix

Whisk together all ingredients in a large mixing bowl until well blended. Transfer to an 8 x 8- inch baking dish that has been sprayed with cooking spray. Bake in preheated 350 degree oven for 45 minutes, until golden.

By Hinda Silber

Broccoli Soufflé Pudding

This recipe can be doubled easily. Great for company!

Yield: 6 servings.

> 1 6-oz. package potato pancake mix
> 2 cups water
> ¾ bunch broccoli, cooked, drained and coarsely chopped
> 4 eggs
> ¼ cup margarine, melted

1 Place potato pancake mix and water in a large mixing bowl. Let stand for 10 minutes.

2 Add remaining ingredients and mix thoroughly with a wooden spoon. Pour mixture into an 8 x 8-inch baking dish that has been sprayed with cooking spray. Bake in preheated 350 degree oven for 30 to 40 minutes, until golden.

By Helen Chapnick

Cheddar, Mushroom and Broccoli Casserole

Yield: 8 servings.

> 1 large bunch broccoli, cut into florets
> 1 tbsp. butter or margarine
> 1 tsp. minced fresh garlic
> 1 cup sliced mushrooms
> 1 10-oz. can condensed cream of mushroom soup
> 1 cup grated Cheddar cheese
> 1 2.8-oz. can French-fried onions

1 In a vegetable steamer, cook broccoli until tender crisp, about 4 to 5 minutes. Drain and plunge broccoli into ice water for 30 seconds to preserve the bright green colour. Drain well and set aside.

2 In a medium skillet, melt butter or margarine over medium heat. Add garlic and mushrooms and sauté for 2 to 3 minutes. Add undiluted soup and mix thoroughly with a wooden spoon.

3 Place broccoli in a 7 x 11-inch baking dish that has been sprayed with cooking spray. Pour mushroom mixture evenly over the broccoli. Sprinkle with cheese and spread French-fried onions over top.

4   Bake in preheated 350 degree oven until cheese melts and onions are lightly browned, about 20 to 25 minutes.

By Linda Waks

Drunken Mushroom Strudel

Yield: 8 to 10 servings.

2 tsp. butter
1 medium shallot, finely chopped
1 medium onion, finely chopped
1 kg. (about 2 lbs.) assorted wild mushrooms
    (shitake, portobello, morel, oyster), thinly sliced
½ cup best quality (vintage) Port
1 tsp. maple syrup
1 tsp. balsamic vinegar
1 tsp. dried thyme
1 tsp. black pepper
1 1-lb. package phyllo pastry
½ cup melted butter (for brushing the phyllo)

This recipe makes two scrumptious strudels. Excellent for company! You will need to use 16 sheets of phyllo dough for this recipe. Any left-over phyllo dough can be refrigerated for 2 to 3 weeks if it is well wrapped.

1   In a large skillet, heat butter over medium heat. Add shallot and onion and sauté until translucent, about 3 to 4 minutes. Add mushrooms, Port, maple syrup, vinegar, thyme and pepper. Cover and cook over medium heat about ½ hour, until most of the liquid has evaporated. Stir occasionally. Remove from heat and let cool.

2   Place one sheet of phyllo pastry on a sheet of parchment paper. Brush lightly with melted butter. Repeat process with 7 more phyllo sheets, stacking one on top of the other.

3   Spoon half the mushroom mixture along one long edge of phyllo, leaving a 1-inch border at bottom and both sides. Roll up phyllo, turning in ends. Brush lightly with butter. Transfer parchment paper and dough onto a cookie sheet.

4   Repeat with remaining phyllo pastry, butter and mushroom mixture. Bake strudels in preheated 325 degree oven for 15 to 20 minutes, until golden.

By Lise Wolfson

Carrot Pudding

If desired, substitute 1 cup craisins (dried cranberries) for the raisins and currants.

Yield: 8 servings.

½ cup vegetable shortening
½ cup brown sugar
1 egg
1 cup grated carrots
½ cup raisins
½ cup currants
1¼ cups flour
1 tsp. baking powder
½ tsp. salt
½ tsp. cinnamon
½ tsp. nutmeg
½ tsp. baking soda
1 tbsp. water

1 In a large mixing bowl, combine shortening, brown sugar and egg with a fork. Add carrots, raisins and currants and mix with a wooden spoon. Add the next 5 ingredients and mix until blended.

2 Dissolve baking soda in water. Add to ingredients. Pour into 7 x 11-inch baking dish that has been sprayed with cooking spray. Bake in preheated 350 degree oven for 1 hour.

By Suzanne Shuchat

Carrot Soufflé

This recipe doubles easily for a crowd. If you are feeling lazy, don't bother separating the eggs. The soufflé won't rise as much but it will still taste delicious. The cornflake topping adds a delightful touch.

Yield: 8 servings.

1 cup cornflakes, lightly crushed
½ cup brown sugar (divided)
2 lbs. cooked carrots (baby carrots or regular carrots, cut in chunks)
½ cup butter, softened
6 tbsp. flour
½ tsp. nutmeg
6 eggs, separated

1   Combine cornflakes with 2 tbsp. of brown sugar in a small bowl. Sprinkle half the mixture into the bottom of a 2-quart soufflé dish or a 9 x 13-inch baking dish that has been sprayed with cooking spray.

2   Place carrots in the work bowl of a food processor or a blender. Process about 10 seconds, or until puréed. Add butter and process another 5 seconds. Add flour, remaining sugar and nutmeg and process another 5 seconds. Add egg yolks and blend another 10 seconds, until thoroughly blended. Pour mixture into large mixing bowl.

3   Place egg whites in another large bowl. Beat by hand or with an electric mixer until light peaks form. Gently fold half the whites into carrot mixture with a rubber spatula. Stir lightly to blend. Gently fold in remainder of the whites. Pour into the prepared baking dish. Top with remaining crumb mixture. Bake in preheated 350 degree oven for 1½ hours.

   By Linda Waks

Springtime Green Peas

Yield: 2 servings.

> 1 lb. fresh green peas, shelled (about 1 to 1¼ cups)
> 2 tsp. vegetable oil
> 2 green onions, thinly sliced, green parts removed
> 1 cup vegetable broth
> 1 tsp. prepared mustard
> ¼ tsp. pepper
> ½ cup evaporated skim milk
> 1 tbsp. cornstarch

1   Fill a saucepan with 2 inches of water and bring to a boil over medium heat. Place vegetable steamer in the pan. Fill with peas. Steam 5 to 7 minutes. Transfer peas to a mixing bowl.

2   In a medium skillet, heat oil over medium heat. Add onions and sauté for 2 minutes. Add broth and cook 1 to 2 minutes. Remove from heat. Whisk in mustard and pepper.

3   In a small bowl, whisk together milk and cornstarch until well blended. Gradually whisk mixture into mustard sauce. Pour over peas and stir with a wooden spoon until well mixed.

   By Rona Cappell

Scalloped Eggplant

Yield: 4 to 6 servings.

4 cups water
1 medium eggplant, peeled and cut in ½-inch cubes
3 tbsp. butter or margarine
3 tbsp. flour
1 medium onion, finely chopped
3 large tomatoes, cored, seeded and cut in ½-inch cubes
2 tsp. salt
1 tbsp. brown sugar
1 cup shredded Cheddar cheese
½ cup bread crumbs

1 In a large saucepan, bring water to a boil over medium heat. Add eggplant and cook for 8 to 10 minutes. Drain well. Transfer to a baking dish that has been sprayed with cooking spray.

2 In a small saucepan, melt butter over low heat. Gradually whisk in the flour until a smooth paste is formed. Add the onion and tomatoes and stir until blended. Sprinkle with salt and brown sugar and blend well. Continue to cook 1 to 2 minutes more, or until paste is thick.

3 Spread paste evenly over eggplant. In a small bowl, combine cheese with bread crumbs. Sprinkle over eggplant. Bake in preheated 350 degree oven for 30 minutes.

By Rina Rosenberg

NOTES:

Angela's Eggplant Romano

Yield: 8 servings.

TOMATO SAUCE
2 tsp. olive oil
1 small onion, finely chopped
2 tsp. minced fresh garlic
1 19-oz. can plum tomatoes (undrained)
1 tbsp. tomato paste
½ tsp. dried basil
½ tsp. dried oregano
½ tsp. salt
1 tsp. pepper
1 tsp. sugar
⅛ tsp. red pepper flakes

1   In a large skillet, heat oil over medium heat. Add onion and garlic and sauté 3 to 5 minutes, or until softened.

2   Reduce heat to medium-low. Add tomatoes, tomato paste and seasonings. Cover and simmer until sauce is thick, about 1 hour. Stir occasionally.

EGGPLANT
1 large eggplant, peeled and thinly sliced into rounds
1 recipe Tomato Sauce (above)
2 cups grated Romano cheese
1 to 2 tbsp. bread crumbs
1 to 2 tbsp. grated Parmesan cheese

1   Stack slices of eggplant in three piles on a plate. Place a sheet of wax paper over the slices. Place a heavy object (e.g., a can of beans) on top of each stack. Let sit for 2 hours while the bitter juices drain from the eggplant. Rinse eggplant slices and pat dry.

2   Place ¼ of the sauce in the bottom of a 7 x 11-inch baking dish that has been sprayed with cooking spray. Arrange ¼ of the eggplant slices in a layer over the sauce. Sprinkle with ¼ of Romano cheese. Repeat 3 more times.

3   In a small bowl, whisk together bread crumbs and Parmesan cheese. Sprinkle over top. Bake in preheated 350 degree oven for 1 hour.

By Renée Stein

Stuffed Eggplant

Serve this dish as a lunch entrée or as a side dish with dinner.

Yield: 4 servings.

2 large eggplants, cut in half lengthwise
2 tbsp. vegetable oil
1 large onion, finely chopped
2 tsp. minced fresh garlic
2 tbsp. additional vegetable oil
1 lb. mushrooms, thinly sliced
1 cup chopped fresh parsley
4 tbsp. bread crumbs
4 tbsp. grated Parmesan cheese

1 Scoop out the pulp from each eggplant half, leaving a firm shell. Cut eggplant pulp into small chunks.

2 In a large skillet, heat 2 tbsp. oil over medium heat. Add onion and sauté for 2 to 3 minutes. Add eggplant and garlic and sauté until eggplant is softened, about 5 minutes. Transfer eggplant mixture to a large mixing bowl.

3 In the same skillet, heat 2 tbsp. oil over medium heat. Add mushrooms and sauté 2 to 3 minutes. Add to eggplant mixture. Stir in parsley.

4 Fill eggplant shells with equal amounts of eggplant mixture. Place on a cookie sheet that has been sprayed with cooking spray. Bake uncovered in preheated 350 degree oven for 1 hour.

5 Remove from oven and sprinkle with bread crumbs and cheese. Return to oven and bake another 5 to 7 minutes.

By May Cappell

Oriental Celery

Yield: 8 servings.

6 cups water

4 cups celery, cut in 1-inch chunks

1 10-oz. can water chestnuts, drained and thinly sliced

1 10-oz. can cream of mushroom soup, undiluted

¼ cup chopped pimento

½ cup bread crumbs

¼ cup slivered almonds, toasted

2 tsp. butter or margarine, melted

1 In a large saucepan, bring water to a boil. Add celery and cook on medium heat until tender, about 5 to 7 minutes. Drain well and transfer to a mixing bowl.

2 Add water chestnuts, soup and pimento to celery and mix thoroughly with a wooden spoon. Pour into a 7 x 11-inch baking dish that has been sprayed with cooking spray.

3 In a small bowl, mix bread crumbs and almonds with butter. Sprinkle over casserole. Bake in preheated 350 degree oven for 25 minutes, until golden.

By Mrs. J. A. Griss

Spinach Casserole

Yield: 6 to 8 servings.

2 cups sour cream

1 package onion soup mix

3 10-oz. packages frozen chopped spinach, cooked and well-drained

1 In a large bowl, whisk together sour cream and onion soup. Add the spinach and stir until blended.

2 Transfer to a 1½-quart baking dish that has been sprayed with cooking spray. Bake uncovered in preheated 350 degree oven for 20 to 25 minutes, until heated through.

By Eleanor Long

Cauliflower Casserole

Yield: 9 servings.

3 eggs

½ cup water

2 tbsp. margarine, melted

½ cup mayonnaise or salad dressing

3 tbsp. flour

3 tbsp. onion soup mix

1 tsp. garlic powder

1 large cauliflower, cooked and mashed (about 3 cups)

¼ cup cornflake crumbs

1   In a large mixing bowl, whisk together first 7 ingredients. Add cauliflower and stir until thoroughly blended.

2   Pour into an 8 x 8-inch square baking dish that has been sprayed with cooking spray. Sprinkle with cornflake crumbs. Bake uncovered in preheated 350 degree oven for 30 minutes.

By Ann Tobe

Marinated Green Beans

Yield: 6 to 8 servings.

1 lb. green beans, ends trimmed

1 lb. yellow beans, ends trimmed

4 tbsp. raspberry vinegar

1 tbsp. Dijon mustard

½ cup olive oil

Salt and pepper to taste

1   Fill a large saucepan with 2 inches of water and bring to a boil over medium heat. Place vegetable steamer in the pan. Fill with beans and steam for 3 to 5 minutes. Plunge beans into cold water. Keep refreshing beans with cold water until they are cold. Transfer to a large mixing bowl.

2   In a small mixing bowl, whisk together vinegar and mustard. Gradually add oil and whisk until blended. Pour over beans. Season with salt and pepper to taste.

By Faith White

Spicy String Beans

Yield: 4 servings.

1 lb. green beans, ends trimmed
½ tsp. vegetable oil
1 tbsp. sesame seeds
2 tbsp. hoisin sauce
1 tbsp. soy sauce
1½ tsp. Thai-style garlic chili sauce
3 tbsp. water
2 tsp. cornstarch
2 green onions, thinly sliced

1 Fill a saucepan with 2 inches of water and bring to a boil over medium heat. Place vegetable steamer in the pan. Fill with beans. Steam for 3 to 5 minutes. Transfer beans to a mixing bowl.

2 In a small skillet, heat oil over medium heat. Add sesame seeds and sauté for 2 minutes, until golden. Transfer to a small bowl.

3 Return skillet to medium heat. Add hoisin sauce, soy sauce and chili sauce and cook 1 to 2 minutes.

4 In a small bowl, whisk together water and cornstarch. Add to skillet and stir until blended. Cook sauce 2 minutes longer, or until thickened.

5 Add beans and continue to cook over medium heat until sauce coats all the beans. Add green onions and remove from heat. Transfer to a serving bowl and sprinkle with sesame seeds.

By Rona Cappell

Green beans used to contain an inedible string, but modern hybrids are stringless, thank goodness.

Asparagus with Caramelized Onions

Caramelized onions are so versatile. They can accompany a main course or spice up a sandwich. Use them as a pizza topping or to stuff a baked potato.

Yield: 2 servings.

1 tbsp. olive oil
2 large onions (about 2 cups), thinly sliced
1 tsp. minced fresh garlic
2 tbsp. sugar
2 tsp. white wine vinegar
¼ tsp. salt
¼ tsp. pepper
2 cups water
8 small asparagus spears

1   In a large skillet, heat oil over medium heat. Add onions and garlic and sauté for 5 minutes. Reduce heat to low. Cover and cook another 10 to 15 minutes.

2   Remove lid and add sugar, vinegar, salt and pepper. Continue to cook another 3 to 5 minutes, stirring constantly, until sauce is thickened and onions are golden brown.

3   Meanwhile, in a large skillet, heat water over medium heat. Add asparagus and cook 3 minutes, until tender. Drain, rinse and transfer to a serving platter. Garnish with caramelized onions.

By Marlene Borins

Squash and Apple Casserole

Yield: 8 servings.

1 medium butternut squash (about 2 lbs.), peeled and
   thinly sliced, seeds removed
4 to 6 Spy apples, peeled, cored and cut in rounds
3 oz. butter or margarine, melted
⅓ cup brown sugar

1   Place sliced squash in a 9 x 13-inch baking dish that has been sprayed with cooking spray. Top with sliced apples.

2   Drizzle melted butter over top. Sprinkle with brown sugar. Bake in preheated 350 degree oven for 1 hour.

By Sandy Hausman

Zaidy Jack's Marinated Roasted Root Vegetables

Yield: 4 to 6 servings.

MARINADE

⅓ cup balsamic vinegar

2 tsp. minced fresh garlic

½ tsp. dried basil

½ tsp. dried thyme

⅓ cup olive oil

Salt and pepper to taste

In a mixing bowl, whisk together first 4 ingredients. Gradually add oil and whisk until blended. Sprinkle with salt and pepper.

VEGETABLES

4 medium potatoes, cut in ½-inch cubes

2 medium carrots, cut in ½-inch cubes

1 medium parsnip, cut in ½- inch cubes

1 large Videlia onion, cut in quarters and held
   together with toothpicks

¾ cup cauliflower florets

¾ cup broccoli florets

½ cup small mushrooms

1 recipe Marinade (above)

1 Line a large cookie sheet with tinfoil. Place half of the marinade in a bowl with the potato, carrot and parsnip cubes. Mix well. Place on cookie sheet in a single layer. Roast uncovered in preheated 400 degree oven for 20 minutes.

2 Place remaining marinade in a bowl with the onion wedges, cauliflower, broccoli and mushrooms. Mix well. Add to vegetables on cookie sheet and continue cooking for 30 minutes, turning occasionally.

By Jack Borenstein

Baked Fennel

Yield: 6 to 8 servings.

4 cups water
2 medium fennel bulbs (about 2 lbs.), thinly sliced
1 tbsp. vegetable oil
3 tsp. minced fresh garlic
1 cup finely chopped onions
4 cups tomato sauce
¼ cup chopped fresh dill
1 cup shredded low-fat Mozzarella cheese

1 In a large saucepan, bring water to a boil over medium heat. Add fennel and cook until tender, about 5 to 7 minutes. Drain and set aside.

2 In a large skillet, heat oil over medium heat. Add garlic and sauté 1 minute. Add onions and sauté 2 to 3 minutes. Add tomato sauce and dill. Reduce heat to low and simmer 10 minutes, stirring occasionally.

3 Pour half of the sauce into a 7 x 11-inch baking dish that has been sprayed with cooking spray. Spread fennel evenly over sauce. Top with remaining sauce. Sprinkle with cheese. Bake in preheated 350 degree oven for 20 minutes, until cheese has melted.

By Marlene Borins

Savory Turnips

Substitute squash, parsnips or carrots for the turnips. This recipe is also delicious with any combination of root vegetables.

Yield: 4 servings.

3 tbsp. butter or margarine
1 cup vegetable broth
3 tbsp. maple syrup
1½ lbs. white turnips, peeled and cut in half
1 tsp. Dijon mustard
Salt and pepper
1 tbsp. chopped fresh parsley

1 In a large saucepan, melt butter or margarine over medium heat. Add vegetable broth and maple syrup and bring to a boil. Add turnips. Reduce heat to medium-low and cook until tender, about 10 to 20 minutes, depending on size.

2   Remove turnips from broth with a slotted spoon and set aside. Do not discard broth. Increase heat to medium and boil the broth on medium heat until it has reduced by half, about 2 to 4 minutes. Whisk in the mustard. Return turnips to saucepan and coat with the sauce. Sprinkle with salt, pepper and parsley.

By Rona Cappell

Zucchini and Carrot Latkes

Yield: 1 dozen.

1 cup shredded potatoes
2 cups grated zucchini
1 cup shredded carrots
½ cup shredded onions
3 eggs, lightly beaten
½ cup matzoh meal
1 tsp. salt
½ tsp. pepper
¼ cup chopped fresh parsley
Vegetable oil for frying

Add some crumbled feta cheese or goat cheese to these latkes to make them even more delicious.

1   Place shredded potatoes, zucchini, carrots and onions in a large colander. Using paper towels, pat out as much excess moisture as you can.

2   In a large mixing bowl, whisk together eggs, matzoh meal, salt and pepper. Fold in vegetables. Add parsley and stir with a wooden spoon until just blended.

3   In a large heavy skillet, heat ¼ cup oil over medium heat. Drop mixture from a large spoon into hot oil to form latkes. Cook 6 to 8 minutes on each side, until brown and crispy.

4   Drain latkes on paper towels. Add additional oil as needed to skillet and repeat Step 3 until mixture is used up.

By Elise Mecklinger

New Potatoes with Mint Pesto

Yeild: 4 servings

MINT PESTO

1 bunch mint leaves, washed and dried

2 tsp. minced fresh garlic

½ tsp. salt

½ tsp. pepper

2 tbsp. olive oil

2 to 3 tbsp. water

Place first 4 ingredients in the work bowl of a food processor. Process for 10 seconds. With machine running, gradually add oil through the feed tube and process another 10 seconds, until thoroughly blended. If pesto is too thick, add a little water.

POTATOES

16 red-skinned baby new potatoes, scrubbed and pierced

1 recipe Mint Pesto (above)

1 Place potatoes in a baking dish that has been sprayed with cooking spray. Bake in preheated 400 degree oven for 50 minutes, or until skins are crisp. Cool slightly.

2 Cut potatoes in halves or quarters and place in a large mixing bowl. Toss with pesto, coating all pieces evenly. Let stand for 10 minutes and serve.

By Debra Verk

Mashed Potatoes with Goat Cheese and Basil

To lighten up this dish, substitute low-fat margarine for the butter and 1% milk for the cream. If you don't have a potato ricer, simply mash the potatoes with a hand masher or a fork.

Yield: 6 servings.

6 cups water

2½ lbs. Yukon Gold potatoes, peeled and cut in 2-inch cubes

½ cup goat cheese, crumbled

4 tbsp. butter, melted

¾ cup 10% cream

3 tbsp. minced fresh basil

2 tsp. minced fresh garlic

Salt and pepper to taste

1   In a large saucepan, bring water to a boil over medium heat. Add potatoes and cook until tender, about 20 minutes. Drain well. Pass potatoes through a potato ricer into a large mixing bowl.

2   Add goat cheese and butter to potatoes and mash together with a fork until blended. Gradually add cream and continue to mash until smooth. Add basil, garlic, salt and pepper and mash until blended. Serve immediately.

By Rona Cappell

Roasted Garlic Mashed Potatoes

Yield: 6 servings.

1 head garlic
1 tsp. olive oil
6 cups water
2½ lbs. Yukon Gold potatoes, peeled and cut in 1-inch chunks
⅔ cup half-and-half cream
6 tbsp. butter, melted
Salt and pepper to taste

1   Cut a ½-inch thick slice from the top of the garlic to expose the cloves. Place on a large piece of tinfoil. Drizzle with oil and wrap tightly. Bake in preheated 400 degree oven for 40 minutes, or until soft. Let cool.

2   In a large saucepan, bring water to a boil over high heat. Add potatoes. Reduce heat to medium-low and cook for about 20 minutes, until tender. Drain well. Return potatoes to the pot. Squeeze the garlic cloves from the skins and add to the potatoes. Mash with a potato masher.

3   In a small saucepan, bring half and half to a simmer over low heat. Add to potatoes. Add butter. Mix with a spoon until thoroughly blended. Sprinkle with salt and pepper to taste.

By Queenie Nayman

Potato and Parmesan Gratin

Yield: 6 servings.

2½ lbs. Yukon Gold potatoes, thinly sliced
Salt and pepper to taste
¼ cup melted butter or margarine
2 cups freshly grated Parmesan cheese
2 cups whole or 2% milk

1   Place ⅓ of the potato slices on the bottom of a 7 x 11-inch baking dish that has been sprayed with cooking spray. Sprinkle with salt and pepper. Drizzle ⅓ of the melted butter over the potatoes. Top with ⅓ of the cheese.

2   Repeat this process 2 more times, ending with the cheese. Drizzle milk over top.

3   Bake in preheated 400 degree oven for 15 minutes. Reduce to 350 degrees and continue to bake for about 60 minutes, or until top is golden brown and most of the milk is absorbed. Let stand for 10 minutes before serving.

By Shari Borenstein

Potato Casserole

Yield: 8 servings.

6 large potatoes, cooked and grated
1⅓ cups sour cream
1 small bunch green onions, thinly sliced, green parts removed
1½ cups shredded Cheddar cheese, divided
1½ tsp. salt
¼ tsp. pepper
Paprika

1   In a large bowl, mix together potatoes, sour cream, onions, 1 cup of cheese, salt and pepper.

2   Place in a 9 x 13-inch baking dish that has been sprayed with cooking spray. Top with remaining cheese and sprinkle with paprika. Bake in preheated 300 degree oven for 30 to 40 minutes, until golden.

By Honey Sherman

Noodle Pudding

Yield: 12 servings.

½ cup sugar

5 eggs

⅓ cup oil

1 10-oz. can pineapple tidbits (do not drain)

1 28-oz. jar applesauce

1 tbsp. lemon juice

1 tsp. vanilla

½ cup raisins (optional)

1 900-gram package medium noodles

½ cup cornflakes, crushed

¾ cup brown sugar

1 tbsp. cinnamon

1   In a large mixing bowl, whisk together sugar, eggs, oil, pineapple (with its juice), apple-sauce, lemon juice, vanilla and raisins.

2   Cook noodles according to package directions. Drain well and add to wet mixture. Pour into 9 x 13-inch baking dish that has been sprayed with cooking spray.

3   In a small bowl, whisk together cornflakes, brown sugar and cinnamon. With a spoon, press mixture down on top of noodle mixture. Bake in preheated 350 degree oven for 45 to 50 minutes.

By Debbie Goldstein

NOTES:

Well-Dressed Potato Skins

Top these crispy treats with salsa, sour cream and/or guacamole.

Yield: 2 dozen.

6 medium potatoes
¼ cup olive oil
Salt, pepper and paprika to taste
½ cup shredded Mozzarella, Cheddar, or
    Monterey Jack cheese (if desired)

1 Prick the skins of the potatoes and wrap each one in tinfoil. Bake in preheated 425 degree oven for 1 hour. Cut each potato into quarters lengthwise. Scoop out pulp to within ½ inch of the skins. Save pulp for mashed potatoes.

2 Brush oil on the outside and inside of each potato skin. Place skins on a baking sheet that has been sprayed with cooking spray. Sprinkle skins with salt, pepper and paprika. Sprinkle with cheese, if desired. Bake in preheated 400 degree oven for 15 minutes, or until skins turn crispy.

By Esther Mecklinger

Vegetable Kugel

Yield: 10 to 12 servings.

1 tsp. oil
1 medium onion, finely chopped
4 cups veggies (any combination of broccoli florets,
    cauliflower florets and zucchini slices)
1 medium carrot, grated
2 tbsp. minced fresh parsley
4 eggs, lightly beaten
½ cup oil
1 cup flour
1 tsp. baking powder
¼ cup cornflake crumbs

1 In a small skillet, heat oil over medium heat. Sauté onion for 2 to 3 minutes. Place in a large mixing bowl.

2 Add veggies, carrot and parsley to the onion. Whisk together eggs and oil and add to veggies. Add flour and baking powder and mix thoroughly.

3 Place in 9 x 13-inch baking dish that has been sprayed with cooking spray. Sprinkle cornflake crumbs over top. Bake in preheated 350 degree oven for 50 minutes, until golden.

By Hinda Silber

Farfel, Chicken and Vegetable Kugel

Yield: 8 to 10 servings.

> 3 cups matzoh farfel
> 2 cups chicken broth
> 3 tbsp. oil
> 2 onions, finely chopped
> 1 tsp. minced fresh garlic
> 2 stalks celery, thinly sliced
> 1 cup mushrooms, thinly sliced
> ½ green pepper, finely chopped
> 2 cups cooked chicken, cut in bite-sized pieces
> 3 eggs, lightly beaten
> Salt, pepper and paprika

1 Combine farfel and broth in a large mixing bowl.

2 In a large skillet, heat oil over medium heat. Add onions, garlic, celery, mushrooms and green pepper. Sauté 2 to 3 minutes. Add chicken and sauté 2 minutes longer.

3 Add mixture to farfel and combine. Add eggs and stir until blended. Sprinkle with salt, pepper and paprika. Transfer to a 2-quart baking dish that has been sprayed with cooking spray.

4 Bake in preheated 350 degree oven for 1 hour, until golden.

By Suzanne Shuchat

In the Thick of It

Pasta Puttanesca

Yield: 4 servings.

5 medium tomatoes, quartered
1 medium red pepper, quartered
1 head garlic, unpeeled, separated into cloves
1 tbsp. olive oil
Salt and pepper to taste
½ cup Niçoise olives, cut in ¼-inch cubes
½ cup green olives, cut in ¼-inch cubes
3 tbsp. capers
2 anchovies, cut in small pieces
4 cups salted water
1 lb. cappellini, fettuccine or pappardelle

1   Place tomatoes, red pepper and garlic in an ungreased 9 x 13-inch glass baking dish. Drizzle olive oil over top. Sprinkle with salt and pepper. Bake for 40 to 45 minutes, or until veggies have shrivelled.

2   Place tomatoes and red pepper in the work bowl of a food processor. Add garlic, squeezing contents of each clove into the bowl. Process for 1 minute, or until puréed.

3   In a large skillet, heat puréed tomato mixture over medium-low heat. Add olives, capers and anchovies. Reduce heat to low and cook for another 5 minutes.

4   Meanwhile, in a large saucepan, bring water to a boil. Add the cappellini and boil until tender, about 7 minutes. Drain in colander. Rinse under cold water. Drain again.

5   Place pasta on a serving platter. Pour sauce over top.

By Elise Mecklinger

NOTES:

Pasta with Roasted Tomatoes and Black Olives

Yield: 4 servings.

12 plum tomatoes, cut in half lengthwise
¼ cup olive oil
1 tbsp. minced fresh garlic
½ cup oil-packed sun-dried tomatoes, cut in julienne strips
¼ tsp. red pepper flakes
½ cup chopped fresh basil
4 cups salted water
1 lb. fusilli (spiral pasta)
12 Kalamata olives, pitted and quartered
¼ cup freshly grated Parmesan cheese

1   Place tomatoes skin side down on a foil-lined cookie sheet. Roast in a preheated 400 degree oven for 30 minutes. Cool slightly. Peel and set aside.

2   In a large skillet, heat oil over medium heat. Add the roasted tomatoes, garlic, sun-dried tomatoes and red pepper flakes. Sauté 2 to 3 minutes. Add basil and cook 1 more minute.

3   In a large saucepan, bring water to a boil. Add fusilli and cook until tender, about 6 minutes. Drain well. Transfer to a large mixing bowl. Add sauce, olives and cheese and toss until combined.

By Debra Verk

NOTES:

Penne à la Shanea

Yield: 4 servings.

3 tbsp. olive oil
1 medium onion, finely chopped
5 tsp. minced fresh garlic
1 cup finely chopped sun-dried tomatoes
½ cup dry white wine
1 28-oz. can plum tomatoes, drained and chopped
1 tbsp. minced fresh basil
1 tbsp. minced fresh oregano
½ tsp. salt
¼ tsp. pepper
4 cups salted water
1 lb. penne
1 bunch broccoli, cut into florets

1   In a large skillet, heat oil over medium heat. Sauté onion and garlic for 2 to 3 minutes. Add sun-dried tomatoes and cook 2 minutes longer. Reduce heat to medium-low. Add wine and simmer about 3 minutes.

2   Add tomatoes, basil, oregano, salt and pepper. Bring to a boil. Reduce heat to simmer and cook about 20 minutes, or until sauce thickens.

3   Meanwhile, in a large saucepan, bring water to a boil. Add the pasta and boil until tender, about 6 minutes. Add broccoli and cook another 3 minutes, or until broccoli is tender. Drain well. Place in large mixing bowl.

4   Toss with sauce and serve.

By Shanea Rakowski

Sauce Bolognese

Yield: 6 servings.

3 tbsp. olive oil
1 medium onion, finely chopped
2 tsp. minced fresh garlic
1 carrot, finely chopped
1 stalk celery, finely chopped
½ tsp. dried rosemary
½ tsp. dried thyme
1 tbsp. chopped fresh parsley
1 lb. lean ground beef
½ lb. ground veal
1 28-oz. can puréed plum tomatoes
¼ cup tomato paste
1 cup beef broth plus 2 beef bouillon cubes
1 tsp. salt
Pinch red pepper flakes
Pepper to taste

1   In a large pot, heat oil over medium-low heat. Add onion and garlic and sauté 5 minutes. Add carrot, celery, rosemary, thyme and parsley and cook another 8 minutes.

2   Add ground beef and veal. Cook until no longer pink, about 8 minutes, stirring often to break up meat.

3   Add tomatoes, tomato paste, beef broth, bouillon cubes, salt and red pepper flakes. Reduce heat to low.

4   Simmer partially covered for 1 hour, stirring occasionally. If sauce becomes too thick, add more beef broth. Add pepper to taste.

By Debra Verk

Linguine with Zucchini, Tomatoes and Pesto

Yield: 4 servings.

PESTO SAUCE
1 cup fresh basil leaves
½ cup fresh parsley
½ cup grated Parmesan cheese
¼ cup pine nuts
1 clove garlic
¼ to ½ cup olive oil

Place first 5 ingredients in the work bowl of a food processor. Process for 10 seconds. While the machine is running, add oil through the feed tube and process another 10 seconds.

LINGUINE AND VEGETABLES
¼ cup olive oil
2 tsp. minced fresh garlic
3 small green zucchini, cut in ½-inch cubes
3 small yellow zucchini, cut in ½-inch cubes
3 tomatoes, peeled, cored, seeded and cut in ½-inch cubes
3 tbsp. chopped fresh parsley
Salt and pepper to taste
4 cups salted water
1 lb. linguine
1 recipe Pesto Sauce (above)
Grated Parmesan cheese, to taste

1   In a large skillet, heat oil over medium heat. Add garlic and zucchini and cook 2 to 3 minutes, or until tender. Reduce heat to low. Add tomatoes and cook 1 to 2 minutes longer. Stir in parsley. Sprinkle with salt and pepper.

2   Meanwhile, in a large saucepan, bring water to a boil. Add linguine and cook 6 minutes, or until tender. Drain well and transfer to a mixing bowl.

3   Toss pasta with zucchini mixture. Divide pasta among 4 serving plates. Top each with a dollop of pesto and a sprinkling of Parmesan cheese. Serve immediately.

By Sandy Hausman

Linguine with Salmon, Leeks and Dill

Yield: 4 servings.

LINGUINE

4 cups salted water

12 oz. linguine

In a large saucepan, bring water to a boil. Add linguine and boil until tender, about 7 minutes. Drain well and set aside.

SAUCE

2 cups low-fat milk

Salt and pepper to taste

¼ tsp. nutmeg

1½ tbsp. flour

1 tbsp. olive oil

¼ cup grated Parmesan cheese

¼ cup white wine

2 tsp. minced fresh garlic

2 leeks, white part only, thinly sliced in rounds

2 tbsp. shallots, finely chopped

12-oz. salmon fillet, cut in 1-inch chunks

3 tbsp. chopped fresh dill

1 In a small saucepan, whisk together milk, salt, pepper and nutmeg over medium heat, until boiling. Remove from heat.

2 In another saucepan, whisk together flour and olive oil over medium heat, stirring constantly, until a thick paste is formed.

3 Add milk mixture to flour mixture and continue to whisk constantly until a thick sauce is formed, about 5 minutes. Stir in Parmesan cheese until well blended. Remove from heat and set aside.

4 In another saucepan, cook wine, garlic, leeks and shallots over medium heat until leeks are tender, about 2 to 3 minutes.

5 Add milk mixture to wine sauce and thoroughly combine. Add salmon chunks. Cover and cook for another 3 to 4 minutes. Sprinkle with dill. Remove from heat. Pour sauce over pasta. Toss immediately and serve.

By Rona Cappell

Artichokes and Fettuccine Fresca

Yield: 4 servings.

The artichokes make a beautiful presentation set in a nest of fettuccine or are delicious served on their own.

ARTICHOKES

4 medium artichokes
¼ cup lemon juice
¼ cup olive oil
1 small dried chili pepper

1   With a sharp knife, cut off the top third of each artichoke and remove any discoloured outer leaves. Rub cut surfaces immediately with lemon juice.

2   Add remaining ingredients to a large pot of boiling water and drop in artichokes. Reduce heat to simmer and cook 30 minutes, or until a leaf pulls away easily. Drain well upside down.

3   Serve at room temperature drizzled with olive oil and lemon. Alternately, set aside and serve with fettuccine (see below).

FETTUCCINE

1 lb. fresh fettuccine
Juice and grated zest of 4 lemons
5 tbsp. extra-virgin olive oil
3 tbsp. freshly grated Parmesan cheese
3 tbsp. coarsely grated Pecorino cheese
Salt and freshly ground black pepper
¾ cup chopped fresh basil
¼ cup chopped fresh mint

1   Cook pasta according to package instructions. Drain well and return to pot.

2   Meanwhile, whisk together lemon juice and olive oil. Stir in cheeses. They will partially melt into the mixture. Add salt and pepper to taste.

3   Pour sauce over pasta and shake pot until pasta is coated. Stir in basil, mint and lemon zest.

4   Pour into 4 flat soup bowls and garnish with a grind of black pepper, some lemon zest and a sprinkling of fresh basil and mint. Set an artichoke in the centre of each bowl.

By Sara Waxman

Veggie Lasagna

This recipe is a family favourite and is very easy to make. It is especially good for those who are in a hurry and not great in the kitchen! You can prepare this in advance, let it cool and then cut it into squares. Reheat covered at 375 degrees for 20 minutes.

Yield: 6 servings.

1 green pepper, cut in ½-inch cubes
1 red pepper, cut in ½-inch cubes
1 zucchini, sliced in ¼-inch rounds
2 cups mushrooms, thinly sliced
1 tbsp. dried parsley flakes
1 tbsp. dried basil
1 tsp. salt
1 19-oz. can diced tomatoes
2 6-oz. cans tomato paste
3 cups cottage cheese
2 eggs, lightly beaten
1 tsp. salt
½ tsp. pepper
2 tbsp. dried parsley flakes
½ cup grated Parmesan cheese
6 to 8 no-boil lasagna noodles
4 to 6 slices Mozzarella cheese

1 Place first 9 ingredients in a mixing bowl and stir until combined.

2 Place cottage cheese, eggs, salt, pepper, parsley flakes and Parmesan cheese in another mixing bowl and blend well.

3 Place 3 to 4 noodles in the bottom of a 7 x 11-inch baking dish that has been sprayed with cooking spray. Spread half of the cottage cheese mixture over the noodles. Place 2 to 3 slices of Mozzarella on top. Pour half of the veggie mixture over top.

4 Repeat step 3. Bake in preheated 375 degree oven for 30 to 45 minutes. (If desired, cut Mozzarella cheese slices on the diagonal and place on top halfway through the baking time for decoration.)

By Cheryl Graff

Microwave Lasagna

Yield: 8 servings.

1 jar (3 cups) spaghetti sauce
1 14-oz. can whole tomatoes with liquid
½ cup water
1 15½-oz. container ricotta cheese
4 cups shredded Mozzarella cheese, divided
1 beaten egg
¼ tsp. garlic powder
9 uncooked lasagna noodles
3 tbsp. grated Parmesan cheese

This lasagna is so easy to make. It is completely cooked in the microwave. You don't even have to boil the noodles!

1   In a large mixing bowl, combine spaghetti sauce, tomatoes and water. Mix with a large spoon until well blended, breaking up the tomatoes.

2   In a large mixing bowl, combine ricotta cheese, ½ cup Mozzarella, egg and garlic powder. Mix with a large spoon until well blended.

3   Pour ⅓ of the sauce mixture into a microwavable 9 x 13-inch baking dish. Place 3 noodles on top of sauce. Spread half of the ricotta mixture over the noodles. Spread 1 cup of the Mozzarella on top of the ricotta.

4   Repeat the layers (sauce, noodles, ricotta and Mozzarella). Cover with the remaining noodles. Pour the remaining sauce mixture over top.

5   Cover the baking dish with plastic, turning back one corner to vent. Microwave on high power for 8 minutes. Microwave at medium power for 30 to 35 minutes, or until noodles are very tender.

6   Sprinkle the top layer evenly with the Parmesan cheese and the remaining Mozzarella. Cover the dish again with plastic wrap and let stand for 10 minutes before serving.

By Barbara Bregman

Perfect Pizza Crust

2 tsp. sugar
¾ cup warm water (105 to 115 degrees)
1½ tsp. active dry yeast
2 tbsp. olive oil
1 tsp. salt
2 cups all-purpose flour

1 Dissolve sugar in warm water. Sprinkle yeast over top. Leave the yeast mixture in a warm place to proof for 8 to 10 minutes, or until bubbles begin to appear.

2 Stir olive oil and salt into yeast mixture.

3 Place flour in a large mixing bowl. Make a well in the centre; add yeast mixture and stir with a wooden spoon until well blended.

4 Transfer the dough to a floured surface. Lightly flour your hands. Knead the dough until it is no longer sticky, about 5 minutes, adding more flour if necessary.

5 Transfer the dough to a large greased mixing bowl. Cover the bowl with a tea towel and let the dough rise until it has doubled in bulk, about 1 hour.

6 When the dough has risen, place it on a floured surface and punch it down. Cover it with a tea towel and let it rest for 15 to 20 minutes.

7 It is now ready to be shaped, topped and baked. This dough will make a large 16-inch pizza.

By Elise Mecklinger

NOTES:

Pizza with Mushrooms, Onions and Goat Cheese

Yield: one 16-inch pizza.

TOMATO SAUCE
1 tbsp. olive oil
½ cup onions, cut in ¼-inch cubes
1 tsp. minced fresh garlic
1 tbsp. red wine vinegar
2 cups canned or fresh chopped tomatoes
¼ cup vegetable broth
⅛ tsp. red pepper flakes
1 tsp. sugar
1 tsp. chopped fresh basil

PIZZA
1 recipe Pizza Crust (page 104)
1 tsp. olive oil
1 tsp. minced fresh garlic
½ cup purple onion, finely chopped
½ cup thinly sliced mushrooms
2 cups crumbled goat cheese or Mozzarella cheese

Substitute any kind of vegetable for the onions and mushrooms. Leftover grilled vegetables work well.

1   In a large saucepan, heat oil over medium heat. Add onions and garlic and sauté for 3 minutes. Add vinegar and cook 1 minute more.

2   Sir in tomatoes, broth, pepper flakes, sugar and basil. Cover and simmer for 20 minutes. If desired, purée in a blender or food processor.

3   Reserve 1 cup of sauce for the pizza. Use the rest at a later date.

4   Roll out and stretch pizza dough to fit a 16-inch pizza pan that has been sprayed with cooking spray. Pour 1 cup tomato sauce over top. Bake in preheated 475 degree oven for 8 to 10 minutes, or until lightly browned.

5   While pizza dough is baking, heat oil over medium heat in a large skillet. Add garlic, onion and mushrooms and sauté for 2 to 3 minutes.

6   Remove pizza from the oven and top with mushroom mixture. Sprinkle cheese over top.

7   Return pizza to the oven and bake another 8 to 10 minutes, or until the crust is golden. Cut pizza into 12 wedges.

by Elise Mecklinger

Coconut Noodle Toss

Yield: 4 servings

4 quarts salted water
½ lb. spaghetti
2 tbsp. peanut oil
1 cup button mushrooms, thinly sliced
1 cup snow peas, slivered
1 cup purple cabbage, slivered
1 red pepper, cored, seeded and slivered
⅓ cup green onions, thinly sliced
⅓ cup chopped fresh mint
¼ cup chopped fresh basil

1 In a large saucepan, bring water to a boil. Add spaghetti and cook about 6 minutes, or until tender. Drain well, rinse and transfer to a mixing bowl. Stir in oil.

2 Add remaining ingredients to noodles and toss until combined.

¾ cup unsweetened coconut milk
1 tbsp. oyster sauce
1 tsp. Chinese chili sauce
2 tbsp. dry sherry
2 tbsp. soy sauce
¼ tsp. salt
1 tbsp. cornstarch
1 tbsp. water
2 tbsp. peanut oil

1 In a small mixing bowl, whisk together first 6 ingredients until thoroughly blended. Set aside.

2 In another small bowl, whisk together cornstarch and water until blended. Set aside.

3 In a large skillet, heat oil over medium heat. Add noodle mixture and sauté for 3 minutes, or until noodles are heated through. Add the coconut sauce and continue to sauté 2 to 3 minutes, or until sauce begins to boil. Stir in cornstarch mixture and continue to cook another 2 minutes, or until noodles are piping hot.

4 Turn out onto a heated platter or 4 individual serving platters.

By Marla Hertzman

Lemongrass and Cilantro Couscous

Yield: 6 servings.

This recipe is simple, quick and delicious.

2½ cups chicken or vegetable broth
1 stalk lemongrass, finely minced
2 medium shallots, finely chopped
1½ cups couscous
¼ cup finely chopped fresh cilantro
½ cup finely chopped fresh mint
Salt and pepper to taste

1   In a large saucepan, bring broth to a boil. Add lemongrass and shallots. Reduce heat to simmer. Cook 2 to 3 minutes.

2   Stir in couscous. Remove from heat. Cover and set aside until all liquid is absorbed, about 10 minutes. Lightly fluff grains with a fork. Gently stir in cilantro and mint. Add salt and pepper to taste.

By Shanea Rakowski

NOTES:

Twice the Rice

This absolutely fabulous side dish can be prepared ahead of time except for the final step that can be done prior to serving. If desired, add slivered almonds or mandarin orange segments at the end. Heat the mandarin oranges in the microwave to warm them up so as not to cool down the rice.

Yield: 4 to 6 servings.

¼ cup wild rice
1 cup white rice (jasmine or brown rice can also be used)
1 tbsp. oil
1 medium onion, finely chopped
2 cups sliced mushrooms
1 cup chicken or vegetable broth
½ cup orange juice
1 tsp. grated orange rind
½ tsp. dried thyme
Salt and pepper to taste

1 Cook wild rice and white rice in separate saucepans, following package directions. Place in a large mixing bowl.

2 In a large skillet, heat oil over medium heat. Add onion and mushrooms and sauté for 2 to 3 minutes. Add to rice and mix thoroughly. Add remaining ingredients.

3 Place in a 7 x 11-inch baking dish that has been sprayed with cooking spray. Bake uncovered in a preheated 375 degree oven for 30 minutes.

By Marlene Goldbach

My Favourite Oven-Fried Rice

For convenience, this recipe can be frozen.

Yield: 8 to 10 servings.

2 cups rice
¼ cup oil
1 package onion soup mix
3 tbsp. soy sauce
1 8-oz. can water chestnuts, drained (reserve liquid)
1 10-oz. can sliced mushrooms, drained (reserve liquid)
1 green pepper, cut in ½-inch cubes
1 red pepper, cut in ½-inch cubes
1 cup onions, finely chopped
3½ cups liquid (reserved liquid from canned vegetables plus cold water)
Salt and pepper to taste

1 Place all ingredients in a large mixing bowl and mix thoroughly with a wooden spoon. Transfer to a 9 x 13-inch baking dish that has been sprayed with cooking spray.

2 Bake covered in preheated 350 degree oven for 1 hour, or until all liquid is absorbed. (Alternatively, cover with plastic wrap and microwave on high for 25 minutes.)

By Faith White

Asparagus Risotto

Yield: 4 to 6 servings.

5 cups water
1¼ lbs. asparagus, trimmed and cut in 1-inch pieces
3 cups vegetable broth plus 2½ cups cooking liquid from asparagus
2 tbsp. olive oil
1½ cups onions, finely chopped
1½ cups Arborio rice
2 tbsp. butter
¼ cup freshly grated Parmesan cheese
¼ cup freshly shaved Parmesan cheese, to garnish

1 In a large saucepan, bring water to a boil. Add asparagus and cook on medium heat for 3 minutes, or until tender. Reserve 2 ½ cups cooking liquid. Transfer asparagus to a bowl of ice water to cool.

2 In a saucepan, combine vegetable broth with reserved cooking liquid from asparagus. Heat to simmering.

3 In a large skillet, heat oil over medium heat. Add onions and sauté 5 minutes. Add rice and stir for 2 minutes. Reduce heat to low.

4 Stir in ¾ cup of the hot broth, stirring constantly, until it has all been absorbed. Continue to slowly add ¾ cup liquid at a time, stirring often. Be sure that each batch of liquid is absorbed before adding the next batch. (This whole process should take 20 to 25 minutes.)

5 Add asparagus, butter and ¼ cup grated Parmesan cheese. Stir until heated through, about 1 to 2 minutes. Transfer to 4 to 6 individual serving bowls. Garnish with shaved Parmesan cheese.

By Rona Cappell

The Big Story I

Fowl Play and Beefy Tidbits

Lemon Chicken

Yield: 6 servings.

3 lemons
1 cup white wine
2 tsp. minced fresh garlic
2 bunches green onions, thinly sliced, green parts removed
½ tsp. dried rosemary
1 tsp. dried oregano
Pinch salt and pepper
6 5-oz. boneless, skinless single chicken breasts
1 tsp. cornstarch mixed with 2 tbsp. cold water

If you don't have a grill, you can prepare this recipe in the oven by broiling the breasts 6 inches from the heat for 4 to 5 minutes per side.

1 Using a fine grater, grate the zest of the lemons into a mixing bowl, making sure not to use the bitter white part. Squeeze the lemon juice into the bowl.

2 Add next 6 ingredients to the lemon juice, mixing thoroughly with a wire whisk.

3 Lightly pound chicken breasts to flatten. Place in a single layer in a large baking dish. Pour lemon marinade over top. Cover and marinate in the refrigerator for 2 to 8 hours, turning chicken pieces over occasionally.

4 Preheat grill. Remove chicken from marinade. Reserve marinade. Grill chicken until thoroughly cooked, about 5 minutes per side.

5 In a small saucepan, heat marinade over medium heat. Cook until mixture is reduced by half. Whisk cornstarch mixture into mixture to thicken slightly. Spoon sauce over chicken breasts.

By Queenie Nayman

NOTES:

Zesty Garlic Chicken

This easy recipe from "MealLeaniYumm!" by Norene Gilletz reheats and/or freezes well.

Yield: 4 to 6 servings.

3 medium onions, sliced
3½ lbs. chicken, cut up
15 cloves garlic
Pepper, paprika and dried basil to taste
1½ cups tomato sauce
½ cup Szechuan-style duck sauce

1 Place onions on the bottom of a large roasting pan that has been sprayed with cooking spray. Place chicken pieces on top of onions.

2 Crush 3 cloves of the garlic and rub them all over the chicken. Season with pepper, paprika and basil. Pour tomato sauce and Szechuan sauce over top. Scatter remaining garlic cloves around the chicken.

3 Cover pan with foil and bake in a preheated 350 degree oven for 1 hour. Uncover and bake ½ hour longer, basting occasionally with pan juices.

By Leah Aryeh

Sweet Chicken

Yield: 8 servings.

1 8-oz. bottle Italian salad dressing
1 8-oz. bottle Catalina salad dressing
2 tsp. minced fresh garlic
1 tbsp. apricot jam
1 tbsp. orange marmalade
2 chickens, cut up
½ cup chopped fresh dill

1 In a large mixing bowl, whisk together salad dressings, garlic, jam and marmalade. Add chicken and toss to coat. Cover and refrigerate at least 1 hour.

2 Spray a large roasting pan and rack with cooking spray. Place chicken on rack. Sprinkle dill over top. Cover and bake in preheated 350 degree oven for 1 hour. Uncover and continue to cook another half hour, basting frequently.

By Ellen Goldstein

Simple Roast Chicken with Kishka

Yield: 4 to 6 servings.

1 roasting chicken (3 to 4 lbs.)
2 to 3 tsp. minced fresh garlic
1 tbsp. paprika
1½ tsp. kosher salt
Freshly ground black pepper to taste
1 tbsp. oil
1 tbsp. minced fresh rosemary (or 1 tsp. dried)
1 whole onion, peeled
1 piece kishka (about 1 lb.), cut in chunks
Orange juice for basting (optional)

1 Rinse chicken and pat dry. Whisk together next 6 ingredients to make a paste. Rub some of the paste into the cavity of the chicken. Place onion inside cavity. Rub the remainder of the paste all over the outside of the chicken.

2 Spray a roasting pan and rack with cooking spray. Place chicken on rack, breast side up. Roast uncovered in preheated 350 degree oven, calculating 20 minutes per pound. Halfway through cooking time, add kishka to the pan and baste with pan juices. Cook until done, basting often. If more basting liquid is needed, add a few spoonfuls of orange juice to the pan.

3 When chicken is ready, remove from oven. Let stand loosely covered with tinfoil for 5 to 10 minutes. Carve and place on platter with kishka. Drain off pan juices and use a gravy separator to eliminate the fat. Serve immediately or prepare ahead and reheat to serve.

By Linda Waks

Kishka (stuffed derma) is a sausage-shaped stuffing mixture that can be found in the prepared food section of most delicatessens. It is delicious served with gravy as a side dish. As the chicken roasts, the kishka absorbs its juices, enhancing the flavour. When roasting chicken, use the convection cycle, if possible. It makes the skin crispy and brown, yet the meat stays tender and juicy.

NOTES:

Chicken Piccata

Yield: 4 servings.

4 tbsp. olive oil
1 tsp. chopped fresh rosemary
1 tsp. chopped fresh thyme
1 tsp. chopped fresh oregano
4 boneless, skinless single chicken breasts, each sliced into 4 slices
2 tbsp. additional olive oil, divided
2 tbsp. minced shallots
6 tbsp. dry white wine
4 tbsp. fresh lemon juice
Fresh parsley sprigs, to garnish

1 In a small bowl, whisk together oil, rosemary, thyme and oregano.

2 Place chicken in a single layer in a 9 x 13-inch baking dish. Pour marinade over top. Marinate for 1 hour at room temperature.

3 In a large skillet, heat 1 tbsp. oil over medium heat. Sauté chicken slices about 2 minutes per side. Remove from heat and place on a serving platter.

4 In a medium skillet, heat remaining oil over medium heat. Sauté shallots about 1 minute. Gradually add wine and lemon juice. Cook 2 to 3 minutes longer. Pour sauce over chicken. Garnish with parsley.

By Wendy Kert

Herb-Flavoured Chicken Breasts

Yield: 3 servings.

½ cup Italian salad dressing
1 tsp. minced fresh garlic
1 tsp. minced fresh basil
1 tsp. minced fresh oregano
3 large chicken breasts
1 small purple onion, thinly sliced
½ tsp. paprika

1 In a small bowl, whisk together first 4 ingredients.

2   Place chicken breasts in a sprayed baking dish. Pour marinade over top. Place onion slices over top. Cover and refrigerate for 1 to 4 hours.

3   Sprinkle paprika over top and bake uncovered in preheated 350 degree oven for 35 to 40 minutes, until chicken tests done.

   By Miriam Kerzner

Orange Chicken

Yield: 4 to 6 servings.

> 3 lbs. chicken, cut up, skin removed (or chicken
>   breasts with bone, skin removed)
> ½ tsp. garlic powder
> ¾ cup cornflake crumbs
> 1 tbsp. grated orange rind
> ⅛ tsp. salt
> ¼ tsp. pepper
> ½ cup orange juice
> 1 chicken bouillon cube
> ½ cup boiling water
> 4 tbsp. margarine
> ½ cup honey

1   Sprinkle chicken with garlic powder. Let stand 15 minutes.

2   In a small mixing bowl, combine crumbs, orange rind, salt and pepper.

3   Dip chicken into orange juice, then coat with crumb mixture. Press the crumb mixture onto the chicken gently to help it stick better.

4   Place chicken pieces in a pan that has been lined with parchment paper (or spray pan with cooking spray). Bake uncovered in preheated 350 degree oven for 30 minutes.

5   In a large measuring cup, dissolve bouillon cube in boiling water. Add margarine and honey. Stir until margarine is melted. Baste chicken with the honey mixture. Continue cooking another 30 to 50 minutes, until done, basting often.

   By Pearl Weiss

Honey Curry Chicken

Yield: 4 to 6 servings.

⅓ cup vegetable oil
½ cup honey
¼ cup prepared mustard
4 tsp. curry powder
1 chicken, cut in 8 pieces

1 In a small bowl, whisk together oil, honey, mustard and curry powder. Place chicken in a roasting pan that has been sprayed with cooking spray. Pour sauce over top and thoroughly coat the chicken pieces. Place pieces skin side up.

2 Bake uncovered in preheated 375 degree oven for 1 hour, basting often. Turn pieces over and bake another ½ hour, or until golden. Reduce heat to 300 degrees and cover chicken loosely with foil until ready to serve.

By Esterita Rajsky

Tarragon Chicken

This recipe is also great on the barbecue.

Yield: 4 servings.

4 boneless, skinless single chicken breasts
Freshly ground pepper to taste
3 tbsp. regular or low-fat mayonnaise
1 tbsp. Dijon mustard
2 tsp. minced fresh tarragon (or ½ tsp. dried)

1 Lightly pound chicken breasts to flatten them. Sprinkle both sides with pepper.

2 In a small bowl, combine mayonnaise, mustard and tarragon. Spread over both sides of breasts. Let stand at room temperature for 1 hour or cover and refrigerate for several hours.

3 Broil chicken about 6 inches from heat for 4 to 5 minutes on each side.

By Eleanor Long

Hoisin and Orange Glazed Chicken

Yield: 4 to 6 servings.

This mahogany-glazed chicken is bursting with flavour. Serve with steamed rice and stir-fried veggies.

ORANGE MARINADE

3 cups freshly squeezed orange juice

1 tbsp. soy sauce

1 tsp. sesame oil

1 tbsp. minced fresh ginger

In a small bowl, whisk together ingredients for marinade until well blended.

CHICKEN

1 roasting chicken (about 3 to 4 lbs.)

¾ cup hoisin sauce

½ orange, peeled and cut up into small pieces

1-inch piece fresh ginger

1 recipe Orange Marinade (above)

1 Spray a roasting pan and rack with cooking spray. Place chicken on rack, breast side up. With a pastry brush, spread hoisin sauce on the outside of the chicken as well as inside the cavity.

2 Place orange pieces and ginger inside the cavity. Pour marinade over chicken. Refrigerate for at least 1 hour or overnight.

3 Roast uncovered in preheated 450 degree oven for 15 minutes. Reduce heat to 400 degrees and cook 35 to 45 minutes longer, basting every 15 minutes or so. If chicken gets dry, add extra orange juice or water.

4 Let stand 10 to 15 minutes before carving.

By Shanea Rakowski

Ginger Chicken with Asian Slaw

To serve, place the Asian Slaw on a large oval serving platter. Arrange chicken breasts attractively over top.

Yield: 4 to 8 servings.

ASIAN SLAW
¼ cup rice vinegar
2 tbsp. sesame oil
2 tsp. soy sauce
1½ tsp. minced fresh ginger
½ cup vegetable oil
Salt and pepper
1 large Napa cabbage, thinly sliced
1 bunch green onions, thinly sliced
1 red pepper, cut in ½-inch cubes
1 medium carrot, thinly sliced
1 cup honey-roasted peanuts

1   In a medium bowl, whisk together first 4 ingredients. Gradually add vegetable oil and whisk until thoroughly blended. Sprinkle with salt and pepper.

2   Place cabbage, onions, red pepper and carrot in a large mixing bowl and toss until combined. Pour dressing over top and toss until mixed. Cover and refrigerate for up to 3 hours before serving. Do not add peanuts more than half an hour before serving.

CHICKEN
3 eggs
2 tbsp. soy sauce
2 tsp. sesame oil
4 to 8 boneless, skinless single chicken breasts
1½ cups flour
1 tbsp. ground ginger
1 tsp. salt
1 tsp. pepper
3 to 4 tbsp. vegetable oil
2 1-inch pieces fresh ginger, halved lengthwise

1   In a large mixing bowl, whisk together eggs, soy sauce and sesame oil. Add chicken to mixture, turning to coat on all sides. Cover and chill at least 2 hours or overnight.

2   On a flat surface, combine flour, ground ginger, salt and pepper. Dip chicken into flour mixture to coat on both sides.

3   In a large skillet heat oil over medium heat. Add fresh ginger and sauté 1 minute. Add chicken and sauté about 10 minutes per side, until cooked through.

By Heather Gotlieb

Honey Mustard Chicken Breasts

Yield: 3 servings.

2 tbsp. margarine
1 tsp. minced fresh garlic
2 tbsp. Dijon mustard
2 tbsp. honey
¼ cup regular or honey mustard
1 tbsp. curry powder
½ tsp. salt
Juice and rind of half a lime
3 large chicken breasts

This quick and easy recipe is sure to please.

1   In a small saucepan, heat first 8 ingredients over medium-low heat. Reduce heat to low and simmer the sauce mixture for 2 minutes, whisking constantly, until thoroughly blended.

2   Place chicken breasts in a sprayed baking dish. Pour sauce over top. Bake uncovered in preheated 350 degree oven for 35 to 40 minutes, until chicken tests done.

By Miriam Kerzner

NOTES:

Beer-Battered Chicken

Throw your diet out the door for this crispy delight. If desired, cut the chicken into cubes and serve it as an appetizer with plum sauce.

Yield: 8 servings.

2 cups flour
1 12-oz. bottle of beer
¼ cup sesame seeds
1 tsp. minced fresh garlic
2 tbsp. chopped fresh parsley
¼ tsp. salt
¼ tsp. pepper
8 boneless, skinless single chicken breasts
Canola or vegetable oil for frying

1   In a large mixing bowl, whisk together flour and beer, adding beer gradually until batter is thick and smooth.

2   Add sesame seeds, garlic, parsley, salt and pepper to batter and whisk until blended.

3   In a large skillet, heat enough oil over medium heat for shallow deep-frying. (Oil should be about ¼ inch deep). Dip chicken breasts in batter, coating well.

4   Place chicken breasts in hot oil and cook about 4 minutes per side, or until golden brown.

5   Remove from skillet and drain well on paper towels. Serve immediately.

By Rona Cappell

NOTES:

North African Chicken with Couscous

Yield: 4 servings.

3 tbsp. lemon juice
1 tsp. cumin
½ tsp. allspice
½ tsp. cayenne pepper
2 lbs. boneless chicken breasts and thighs, cut into large chunks
2 tbsp. olive oil
1 medium red onion, finely chopped
1 bunch green onions, thinly sliced
2 tsp. minced fresh garlic
2 large sweet potatoes, peeled and cut in ½-inch cubes
2 cups low-fat chicken broth
1 19-oz. can chickpeas, drained and rinsed
½ cup pitted prunes, quartered
1 package couscous mix
½ cup chopped fresh parsley or coriander
¼ cup chopped fresh mint
1 lemon, thinly sliced

1 In a small bowl, whisk together lemon juice, cumin, allspice and cayenne. Place chicken in a large mixing bowl and pour mixture over top. Set aside.

2 In a large skillet, heat oil over medium heat. Add onions, garlic and sweet potatoes. Cook over medium heat for about 5 minutes, stirring constantly.

3 Add chicken and sauté 2 to 3 minutes. Add broth, chickpeas and prunes. Bring to a gentle boil. Reduce heat to low. Cover and simmer until chicken and vegetables are tender, about 10 minutes.

4 Make couscous according to package directions.

5 Transfer couscous to a large serving platter. Pour the chicken mixture over the couscous. Sprinkle with parsley or coriander and mint. Garnish with lemon slices.

By Harriet Bomza

Chicken and Mango Wraps

If desired, wrap each roll in plastic wrap, cover with a damp tea towel and refrigerate for a few hours. For a pretty presentation, cut on the diagonal into thick slices. The salsa can also be used as a delicious accompaniment to fish or as a dip for pita chips.

Yield: 4 servings.

MANGO SALSA
1½ mangos, cut in ½-inch cubes
¼ cup chopped tomatoes
¼ cup green onions, thinly sliced, green parts removed
1 tbsp. finely chopped green pepper
2 tbsp. lemon juice
2 tbsp. orange juice
1 tbsp. minced fresh parsley
1 tsp. minced seeded jalapeno pepper
1 tsp. minced fresh mint

Place all ingredients in a large mixing bowl and thoroughly combine.

CHICKEN WRAPS
¼ cup lemon juice
2 tsp. minced fresh garlic
½ tsp. ground cumin
½ tsp. paprika
½ tsp. pepper
½ tsp. cayenne pepper
½ tsp. salt
¼ cup olive oil
4 boneless, skinless single chicken breasts (about 1 lb.)
4 10-inch flour tortillas

1 In a small bowl, whisk together first 7 ingredients. Gradually add oil and whisk until thoroughly blended.

2 Place chicken in a shallow baking dish. Pour marinade over top. Cover and refrigerate for a few hours, turning chicken occasionally.

3 Preheat grill or barbecue. Cook chicken over medium heat for about 5 minutes per side, or until no longer pink inside. (Or sauté chicken in a large skillet that has been coated with cooking spray for about 5 minutes per side.)

4 When cool, cut chicken on the diagonal into thin slices. Add chicken to salsa and mix well.

5 Divide chicken mixture among tortillas. Roll up each tortilla.

By Elise Mecklinger

left to right: Imitation Crab Crostini, page 10,
Goat Cheese and Pesto Tortilla Pizzas, page 14,
Potato Pancakes with Smoked Salmon Topping, page 12

Southwest Corn Chowder, page 29

Snow Pea and Mango Salad, page 48

Couscous Chicken Salad, page 58

Oriental Steak, page 135, with Spicy String Beans, page 83, and Rainbow Crystal Fold, page 15

Veggie Lasagna, page 102

Cheesecake, page 205

Pretty Pie, page 216

Honey Garlic Chicken Wings

Yield: 4 to 6 servings.

½ cup liquid honey
¼ cup lemon juice
½ cup water
3 tbsp. ketchup
1 tsp. minced fresh garlic
½ tsp. ground ginger
½ tsp. salt
3 lbs. chicken wings (cut each wing into 2 pieces)
¼ cup margarine

1. In a small saucepan, heat honey, lemon juice, water, ketchup, garlic, ginger and salt over medium heat until just boiling. Pour marinade into a mixing bowl.

2. Add wings to the bowl and coat thoroughly. Marinate in the refrigerator for several hours, turning pieces often.

3. Put margarine in a 9 x 13-inch baking dish and place in preheated 400 degree oven for a few minutes, until melted. Remove chicken from marinade, shaking pieces to remove excess liquid. Reserve marinade, refrigerating it until needed.

4. Place wings in baking dish, turning them over in margarine to coat on all sides. Bake uncovered for 25 minutes. Turn pieces over and bake another 20 minutes. Pour reserved marinade over top and bake another 10 minutes.

By Eleanor Long

NOTES:

Cornish Hens with Herbes de Provence

Herbes de Provence is an aromatic mixture of herbs containing basil, fennel seed, lavender, marjoram, rosemary, sage, summer savory and thyme.

Yield: 6 to 8 servings.

1¼ cups olive oil
3 tbsp. lemon juice
4 Cornish hens
Salt and pepper
12 sprigs fresh basil (about ⅓ cup tightly packed leaves)
4 tbsp. Dijon mustard
3 tbsp. balsamic vinegar
4 tsp. minced fresh garlic
1 tbsp. herbes de Provence

1   In a small mixing bowl, whisk together oil and lemon juice. Place Cornish hens in a large mixing bowl. Pour oil mixture over top. Marinate for 3 hours, turning occasionally.

2   Remove hens from marinade, reserving marinade. Sprinkle each hen inside and out with salt and pepper. Place 2 basil leaves in each cavity. Truss each hen. Rub each one with 1 tbsp. mustard.

3   Place hens in a large roasting pan. Roast uncovered in preheated 450 degree oven for 15 minutes.

4   Meanwhile combine the reserved marinade, vinegar, garlic and herbes de Provence. Reduce heat to 350 degrees. Continue to roast about 45 minutes longer, or until juices run clear when thigh is pierced. Baste frequently with marinade mixture during cooking.

By Debra Verk

NOTES:

First Class Duck

Yield: 4 servings.

1 cup chicken broth
¼ cup white wine
¾ cup orange juice
½ cup dates
½ cup dried apricots
½ tsp. cinnamon
½ tsp. ground ginger
1 tsp. sugar
1 tbsp. grated orange zest
2 tbsp. sherry wine vinegar
4 single duck breasts, bone and extra fat removed, skin on
Salt and pepper
1 tbsp. olive oil

1 In a medium saucepan, heat chicken broth, wine and orange juice over medium heat. Bring to a boil. Add dates and apricots. Reduce heat to medium-low and cook about 7 to 10 minutes, or until fruit has softened.

2 Add cinnamon, ginger, sugar, orange zest and vinegar. Whisk until thoroughly blended. Reduce heat to low and simmer 5 minutes.

3 Transfer sauce to a blender and purée until smooth. Set aside.

4 Make 3 slits in the skin of each breast, being careful not to pierce the meat. Season with salt and pepper.

5 In a large skillet, heat oil over medium heat. Sauté breasts on each side for about 8 minutes.

6 Slice each breast into ½-inch slices and place on individual plates. Spoon sauce over top.

By Rona Cappell

Company Turkey with Sausage Herb Stuffing

Yield: 15 to 18 servings.

SAUSAGE HERB STUFFING
¼ cup margarine
2 tsp. minced fresh garlic
2 medium onions, finely chopped
2 stalks celery, thinly sliced
1 cup mushrooms, thinly sliced
6 to 8 cups bread cubes, lightly toasted (or plain croutons)
½ lb. cooked turkey sausage, crumbled (or 1 cup smoked
    chicken or turkey, cut in ½-inch cubes)
1 tsp. paprika
1 tsp. poultry seasoning
1 tsp. salt
1 tsp. pepper
1½ cups chicken broth
½ cup chopped fresh parsley

1 In a large skillet, heat margarine over medium heat. Add garlic, onions, celery and mushrooms and sauté 3 minutes, until softened. Transfer to a large mixing bowl.

2 Add bread cubes or croutons to vegetable mixture. Add turkey sausage (or smoked chicken or turkey), paprika, poultry seasoning, salt and pepper. Mix thoroughly with a wooden spoon.

3 Add broth and parsley and thoroughly combine.

4 Use mixture to stuff turkey (see below). Don't stuff turkey until just before cooking. (Alternatively, you can transfer the stuffing mixture to a baking dish that has been sprayed with cooking spray. Bake in preheated 350 degree oven for 30 to 40 minutes.)

TURKEY
1 large turkey (about 15 lbs.)
1 recipe Sausage Herb Stuffing (above)
2 tbsp. melted margarine
½ tsp. dried sage
½ tsp. paprika
½ tsp. salt
½ tsp. pepper
1 large onion, cut in chunks

1 head garlic (about 15 cloves), papery skins removed
2 stalks celery, cut in chunks
1 parsnip, cut in chunks
1 large carrot, cut in chunks
2½ cups water

1   Remove giblets and neck from the turkey. Rinse it inside and out and dry thoroughly.

2   Stuff the neck cavity with about 2 cups of the stuffing. Fold the loose skin over and sew the opening shut with a trussing needle and heavy white butcher's twine, or use skewers.

3   Stuff the body cavity with the rest of the stuffing. Sew the opening shut or use skewers. Tie the drumsticks together with twine.

4   In a small bowl, whisk together margarine, sage, paprika, salt and pepper. Rub mixture all over the turkey.

5   Place chunks of onion, garlic, celery, parsnip and carrot in the bottom of a roasting pan. Add water. Place rack on top of vegetables. Place turkey on rack breast-side up.

6   Cover turkey with a tent of tinfoil and roast for 4 hours in preheated 325 oven. Baste occasionally with pan juices. Remove foil and roast 1 hour longer, or until juices run clear when thigh is pierced.

GRAVY
4 tbsp. pan drippings
4 tbsp. flour
3½ to 4 cups chicken or turkey broth
1 tsp. sage
1 tsp. poultry seasoning
½ tsp. salt
½ tsp. pepper

In a large saucepan, heat drippings over medium heat. Whisk in flour, stirring until golden. Add broth, sage, poultry seasoning, salt and pepper and continue to whisk until gravy reaches a boil. Remove from heat.

By Elise Mecklinger

Mediterranean Lamb

Yield: 4 servings.

8 lamb chops
3 medium potatoes, thinly sliced
2 10-oz. cans green peas, drained (reserve liquid)
1 14-oz. can stewed tomatoes
1 tsp. dried oregano

1 In a large nonstick skillet, sauté lamb chops in their own juices over medium heat, about 3 to 5 minutes per side. Transfer to a large casserole dish.

2 In the same skillet, sauté potato slices in lamb juices over medium heat, allowing about 2 minutes per side. Place potato slices on top of lamb chops.

3 Add liquid from peas to the pan juices in the skillet and stir well, (serve reserved peas as a side dish.) Pour this mixture over the lamb and potatoes. Pour tomatoes over top and sprinkle with oregano.

4 Bake in preheated 350 degree oven for 30 to 45 minutes, or until meat moves away from the bone easily.

By Wendy Kert

Beef Stew

This stew is wholesome, delicious and easy to prepare. You can also make it with stewing veal. If desired, add 2 cups of fresh or frozen green peas to stew for the last 5 minutes of cooking for colour.

Yield: 4 to 5 servings.

1 tbsp. vegetable oil
1 tsp. minced fresh garlic
1 medium onion, cut in ½-inch dice
2 lbs. stewing beef
1 10-oz. can tomato sauce
1 10-oz. can tomato soup
½ tsp. sugar
1 tsp. paprika
1 tsp. salt
1 tsp. pepper
4 carrots, cut in 1-inch chunks
5 medium potatoes, quartered

1. In a large Dutch oven or stockpot, heat oil over medium heat. Add garlic and onions and sauté 3 minutes, until softened. Remove from pan and set aside. Add beef and sauté about 3 minutes per side. Remove from pan and set aside.

2. Drain fat from pot. Return beef to pot. Add tomato sauce, tomato soup, sugar, paprika, salt and pepper. Reduce heat to low. Cover and simmer for 1 hour.

3. Add carrots and potatoes and continue to simmer for 45 minutes, or until tender.

By Lesley Campbell

Standing Rib Roast – An Unusual Way

Yield: 8 servings.

6 to 6½ lbs. first-cut roast beef
2 tbsp. parve margarine
1 tsp. minced fresh garlic
1 tbsp. dry mustard
1 tbsp. salt

1. Remove beef from the refrigerator and let stand at room temperature at least 3 hours to bring it to room temperature.

2. In a small bowl, combine margarine, garlic, mustard and salt. Using a knife, spread mixture over beef on all sides, including the ends. Place in a roasting pan, fat side up. The ribs form a natural rack.

3. At least 2 hours before serving, preheat oven to 400 degrees. Place beef in lower third of oven. Roast uncovered for 40 minutes.

4. Without opening the oven door, turn the heat down to 200 degrees and continue to cook undisturbed for at least 1 hour for rare, or 2 to 3 hours for medium roast beef.

By Jacquie Kolber

This roast turns out crusty brown on the outside, juicy and rare all the way through. If possible, buy your beef at least 3 or 4 days ahead, as it needs to age for better flavour. To store, loosely wrap in plastic wrap and refrigerate.

Barb's Rosemary Rib Roast

This dish is beautiful when served surrounded by sautéed baby vegetables. Marinate the meat a day ahead for flavourful results.

Yield: 10 servings.

½ cup chopped fresh rosemary
4 tsp. minced fresh garlic
2 tsp. salt
6 tbsp. olive oil
7 to 7½ lbs. well trimmed boneless beef rib roast (no cap)
Rosemary sprigs

1   Place first 3 ingredients in the work bowl of a food processor and process 5 seconds. Add the oil through the feed tube and continue processing for another 5 seconds.

2   Place roast in roasting pan and rub paste all over. Cover and refrigerate overnight.

3   Place roasting pan on the middle rack of the oven. Roast uncovered in preheated 350 degree oven until meat thermometer inserted straight down from the top centre registers 125 degrees for rare (about 1 hour and 45 minutes). Let stand another 30 minutes.

4   Garnish with rosemary sprigs.

By Lesley Binstock Offman

Amazing Fillet of Beef

This recipe is quick, easy, elegant and delicious. The horse-radish-flavoured mayonnaise makes an excellent accompaniment.

Yield: 6 servings.

BEEF
1 fillet of beef (about 3 lbs.)
2 tbsp. olive oil
2 tbsp. Dijon mustard
2 tbsp. minced fresh garlic
Freshly ground pepper
1 package onion soup mix

1   Place roast on a rack in a roasting pan. Smear with oil, then mustard and garlic. Sprinkle with pepper and onion soup mix.

2   Roast uncovered in preheated 500 degree oven for 10 minutes. Reduce heat to 350 degrees and roast another 40 to 45 minutes. Let stand 10 minutes for easier slicing.

HORSERADISH MAYONNAISE

¾ cup parve whipping cream

½ cup mayonnaise

½ cup white horseradish, drained

2 tbsp. Dijon mustard

Pinch sugar

Salt and pepper to taste

1 Place parve whipping cream in the bowl of an electric mixer. Beat on medium-high speed until stiff peaks form. Set aside.

2 In a mixing bowl, whisk together mayonnaise, horseradish and mustard. Fold in whipping cream.

3 Add sugar, salt and pepper and fold in until blended.

By Lesley Binstock Offman

South African Brisket

Yield: 6 servings.

½ large bottle ginger ale (about 4 cups)

1 package dry onion soup mix

1 package dry mushroom soup mix

½ cup chutney or plum sauce

¾ cup tomato sauce

1 beef brisket (about 5 lbs.)

1 tsp. peppercorns

3 bay leaves

For a delicious brisket, make it the day before. Refrigerate it overnight, then slice it. Remove the hardened fat from the sauce and reheat the brisket in the sauce.

1 In a large mixing bowl, blend together first 5 ingredients with a wire whisk.

2 Place brisket on a rack in a roasting pan and pour liquid over top. Sprinkle peppercorns and bay leaves over top.

3 Bake covered in 325 degree oven for 3½ hours, or until tender.

By Dolly Kerzner

Apple Glazed Brisket

Yield: 8 to 10 servings.

> 1 beef brisket (4 to 4½ lbs.)
> 6 cloves garlic, cut in half
> 3 small cooking onions, cut in quarters
> 1 to 2 cups water
> 1 10-oz. jar apple jelly
> ⅓ cup cooking white wine
> 2 tbsp. thinly sliced green onions
> 3 tbsp. prepared mustard
> 1½ tsp. salt
> 1 tsp. pepper
> 1 tsp. to 1 tbsp. curry powder (to taste)

1 Place brisket in a roasting pan. Cut slits in meat and insert garlic cloves. Place the onions around the meat. Pour water into pan, almost to the top of the brisket.

2 Cook covered in preheated 325 degree oven for about 2 hours, or until tender, basting occasionally. When cool, wrap in tinfoil and refrigerate overnight.

3 In a small saucepan, heat apple jelly and wine over medium heat, whisking until smooth. Whisk in onions, mustard, salt, pepper and curry powder and stir until thoroughly blended. Let cool, refrigerate overnight.

4 The next day, unwrap the brisket and slice across the grain. Place brisket slices in the roasting pan and pour sauce over top. Cook covered in preheated 325 degree oven for 30 minutes to 1 hour, until tender, basting occasionally.

By Lil Balsky

My Mother's Brisket Recipe

Yield: 8 to 10 servings.

> 1 beef brisket (4 to 5 lbs.)
> Pepper, dry mustard and garlic powder to taste
> 1 package onion soup mix
> Handful of brown sugar (about ⅓ cup)
> Ketchup (about ⅓ cup)
> Orange juice (about ¾ to 1 cup)
> 8 large potatoes or sweet potatoes, peeled and cut into eighths

1. Place brisket in a roasting pan. Season with pepper, mustard and garlic powder. Sprinkle ¾ of the package of onion soup mix on top of the brisket. Distribute last ¼ of the package in corners around the brisket.

2. Cover the brisket sparingly with brown sugar. Pour ketchup on top of the brisket by outlining the meat and then making an X's and O's design.

3. Pour orange juice around brisket, covering the bottom of the pan. Cover and bake in preheated 350 degree oven for about 3 hours, until tender. Place potatoes around brisket 1 hour before serving. Slice brisket against the grain into thin slices, trimming excess fat.

By Marcy Abramsky

BBQ Brisket

Yield: 8 to 10 servings.

> 1 beef brisket (about 5 lbs.)
> Salt and pepper
> 1 8-oz. bottle Italian salad dressing
> ½ cup ketchup
> ½ cup water
> 1 small onion, finely chopped
> 1 tsp. minced fresh garlic
> 1 tbsp. wine vinegar
> ½ tbsp. Worcestershire sauce
> 1 tbsp. sugar
> 1 tsp. curry powder

1. Place roast on a rack in a roasting pan. Sprinkle with salt and pepper. Pour salad dressing over roast. Cover pan with foil or lid and refrigerate overnight.

2. Bake covered in preheated 350 degree oven for about 3½ hours, basting every 30 minutes. Uncover and bake an additional 30 minutes, or until tender when pierced with a fork.

3. Let cool. Cut roast against the grain into thin slices and place in a baking dish.

4. In a mixing bowl, whisk together remaining 8 ingredients. Pour over sliced brisket. Cover with foil and refrigerate overnight.

5. Heat in preheated 350 degree oven for about 30 minutes or until heated through.

By Honey Sherman

Brisket by Bubbie May

Yield: 12 to 14 servings.

1 large Spanish onion, thickly sliced
1 double brisket (7 to 8 lbs.)
Salt, pepper and garlic powder to taste
1 package dry onion soup mix
Water, as needed

1 Place sliced onions in the bottom of a heavy roasting pan. Season brisket with salt, pepper and garlic powder and place fat-side up on top of onions.

2 Sprinkle meat with onion soup. Add enough water to cover meat halfway. Cover roasting pan and bake in preheated 350 degree oven for 4 hours.

3 Check roast occasionally to make sure that there is enough water in the pan so that the roast will not dry out. The roast is done when a fork is easily inserted through the centre.

GRAVY
2 heaping tbsp. Bisto (gravy powder)
1 cup water

1 Remove brisket from the pan and let cool. Skim off fat from the liquid in the pan and discard.

2 Transfer remaining liquid and onions from roasting pan into a saucepan and bring to a boil over medium heat.

3 In a small mixing bowl, whisk Bisto with water until dissolved. Pour slowly into boiling liquid. Reduce heat to low, stirring constantly, until thickened. Simmer for 5 minutes.

ASSEMBLY

1 Pour ¼ of the gravy in the bottom of a 9 x 13-inch baking dish or serving dish.

2 Slice roast against the grain and place in the dish in its original shape so that it resembles a whole brisket. Pour remaining gravy and onions over top.

3 Cover with foil and refrigerate. This can be made 2 or 3 days in advance, or frozen up to 1 month.

4 To serve, cover with foil and heat in preheated 350 degree oven for 20 to 25 minutes.

By May Cappell

Oriental Steak

Yield: 4 servings.

ORIENTAL MARINADE
¼ cup tamari or light soy sauce
¼ cup rice wine vinegar
¼ cup hoisin sauce
2 tbsp. brown sugar
2 tbsp. vegetable or canola oil
1 tsp. minced fresh ginger
1 tsp. minced fresh garlic

In a mixing bowl, whisk together all ingredients for marinade until thoroughly blended.

STEAK
1½ to 2 lbs. flank steak
1 recipe Oriental Marinade (above)
1 tsp. vegetable or canola oil
1 tsp. minced fresh garlic
¾ cup thinly sliced green onions
2 cups thinly sliced shiitake mushrooms

1   Place steak in a baking dish. Pour marinade over top. Cover and refrigerate overnight.

2   Preheat broiler or barbecue. Broil or barbecue steak 5 to 8 minutes per side. Transfer marinade to a small saucepan and set aside.

3   Meanwhile, in a small skillet, heat oil over medium heat. Sauté garlic, onions and mushrooms for 3 minutes.

4   Bring reserved marinade to a boil over medium heat. Reduce heat to low and add onions and mushrooms. Pour over the steak. Serve immediately.

By Rona Cappell

The Very Best Chili

This dish tastes best if it's made the day before.

Yield: 4 to 6 servings.

1 tbsp. vegetable oil
1 tsp. minced fresh garlic
1 medium onion, finely chopped
1 to 2 lbs. ground beef or veal
2 28-oz. cans chopped tomatoes, drained
2 19-oz. cans kidney beans, drained
1 bay leaf
¾ tsp. salt
1 tsp. sugar
1 tbsp. chili powder
Pinch cayenne pepper

1   In a large stockpot, heat oil over medium heat. Add garlic and onion and sauté for 2 minutes, until softened. Add ground meat and sauté until it loses its pink colour, stirring often.

2   Add tomatoes, beans, bay leaf, salt, sugar, chili powder and cayenne. Cover and simmer for at least 1 hour, stirring occasionally.

By Fran Sonshine

Veal Chops with Dried Fruit

Yield: 4 servings.

1 tbsp. olive oil
4 first-cut veal chops (1 inch thick)
2 medium onions, thinly sliced
1 tsp. minced fresh garlic
½ tsp. ground ginger
1 tsp. soy sauce
1 tsp. Worcestershire sauce
½ cup beef broth
½ cup port wine
½ lb. dried fruit (apricots, apples, prunes)

1 In a large skillet, heat oil over medium heat. Add chops and sauté 2 minutes on each side. Place in large baking dish that has been sprayed with cooking spray.

2 In same skillet, sauté onions and garlic until golden brown, about 2 to 3 minutes. Add the next 5 ingredients and stir until blended.

3 Pour liquid over the chops. Cover with tinfoil. Bake in preheated 350 degree oven for 30 to 40 minutes. Add dried fruit and bake another 15 minutes, or until chops are tender.

   By Dolly Kerzner

Peppercorn Burgers

Yield: 4 servings.

1½ lbs. lean ground beef
Salt to taste
1½ tbsp. crushed black peppercorns
2 tbsp. parve margarine
1½ tbsp. finely minced shallots
⅓ cup dry red wine
1½ tbsp. cognac
½ cup beef broth

1 Shape beef into 4 patties of equal size. Sprinkle both sides of burgers with salt and crushed peppercorns, pressing the peppercorns into the burgers. Refrigerate until ready to cook.

2 Heat a large heavy skillet over medium heat until the pan is very hot. Add the patties and cook 5 minutes on one side. With a spatula, flip the burgers over and cook another 5 minutes. Remove to a platter and loosely cover with tinfoil to keep warm.

3 In the same skillet, heat 1 tbsp. margarine over medium-low heat. Add shallots and stir with a wooden spoon for 2 minutes. Add wine and cook 1 minute longer. Add cognac and cook until sauce is reduced to half, stirring often. Add the beef broth and cook until sauce is reduced to about ⅓ cup. Swirl in remaining margarine.

4 Return burgers to pan and coat with the sauce. Add juices from the platter to the pan. Cook 1 minute longer.

5 To serve, spoon sauce over burgers.

   By Debra Verk

Glazed Meatloaf

It's so easy to turn this tasty meatloaf into Shepherd's Pie! Just spread 1½ cups mashed potatoes over the top of the loaf. Bake an additional 5 to 7 minutes, or until browned.

Yield: 4 servings.

MEATLOAF
1 tsp. olive oil
⅓ cup onion, finely chopped
½ green pepper, finely chopped
1 tbsp. minced fresh garlic
1 lb. ground beef, veal, chicken or turkey (or a mixture)
3 slices bread, torn into small cubes
¼ cup ketchup
1 tsp. salt
1 tsp. pepper
½ tsp. dry mustard

GLAZE
¼ cup ketchup
½ tbsp. white horseradish
1½ tbsp. brown sugar
1 tsp. prepared mustard

1 In medium saucepan, heat oil over medium heat. Add onion, green pepper and garlic and sauté 3 minutes, until softened.

2 Place ground meat, bread, ketchup, salt, pepper and mustard in a large mixing bowl. Blend thoroughly with a wooden spoon. Add onion mixture and combine thoroughly.

3 Transfer to a 9 x 5-inch loaf pan that has been sprayed with cooking spray. Bake in preheated 350 degree oven for 40 minutes.

4 In a small mixing bowl, whisk together ketchup, horseradish, brown sugar and mustard. Spread on top of meatloaf. Bake another 10 minutes.

By Elise Mecklinger

Hoisin Meatballs

Yield: 4 servings as a main course, 6 to 8 servings as an appetizer.

SIMMERING SAUCE

1 cup hoisin sauce

1 tbsp. soy sauce

1 cup apple juice

1½ tsp. sesame oil

1½ tbsp. cooking sherry

1 tsp. minced fresh ginger

In a large saucepan, bring all ingredients to a simmer over medium-low heat.

MEATBALLS

1 lb. ground beef, veal, chicken or turkey (or a combination)

1 egg or 2 large egg whites

¼ cup bread crumbs or cornflake crumbs

¼ cup hoisin sauce

2 tsp. soy sauce

1 tsp. cooking sherry

2 green onions, finely chopped

1 recipe Simmering Sauce (above)

1 Place first 7 ingredients in a large mixing bowl. Blend thoroughly with a wooden spoon. Shape meatballs into walnut-sized balls.

2 Heat Simmering Sauce on low heat. Drop meatballs into sauce and cook about 45 minutes. If meatballs don't fit into a single layer in the pot, stir carefully halfway through cooking.

By Esther Mecklinger

Serve these delicious meatballs over rice as a main dish. They also make perfect little appetizers.

NOTES:

Stove Top Chulent

Chulent is a thick satisfying stew where the starring ingredients are beans and potatoes. A traditional Sabbath lunchtime meal, chulent is often started in a pot on the stove and then transferred to the oven to cook slowly at a low temperature overnight. This version is faster. It's ready in only 3 hours! If you are in the mood for some old-fashioned goodness, try this hearty dish.

Yield: 6 to 8 servings.

2 cups dried beans (a mixture of kidney, navy and/or lima beans)
1 tbsp. oil
1 tsp. minced fresh garlic
2 medium onions, finely chopped
¼ cup flour
1 tbsp. paprika
1 tbsp. salt
¼ tsp. pepper
1½ lbs. flunken (beef short ribs) or stewing beef, cut in chunks
½ cup barley
1 bay leaf
6 cups boiling water
3 large potatoes, cut in eighths

1   Rinse beans well and set aside. If desired, beans can be soaked for an hour to soften. Make sure to reduce the cooking time by about ½ hour.

2   In a large stockpot, heat oil over medium heat. Add garlic and onions and sauté 2 to 3 minutes, until softened.

3   Combine flour, paprika, salt and pepper in a plastic bag. Add meat to the bag and coat with the flour mixture. Add meat to the pot and sauté until browned on all sides, about 5 to 7 minutes.

4   Add drained beans, barley and bay leaf to the pot. Pour boiling water over top. When mixture begins to boil, add potatoes. Reduce heat to low. Cover and simmer for 3 hours. Make sure that the cover is not on too tight. Stir occasionally, adding more water, salt and pepper, if necessary.

5   Remove flunken bones. Serve with thick crusty bread for dunking.

By Linda Waks

Cabbage Rolls

Yield: about 3 dozen.

1 tbsp. olive oil
1 large cooking onion, cut in ¼-inch dice
1 28-oz. can tomatoes
¼ cup ketchup
¾ cup brown sugar
2 tbsp. lemon juice
2½ lbs. mix of ground beef, veal, turkey or chicken
¾ cup raw white rice
Salt and pepper to taste
1 head cabbage, separated into leaves (see sidebar for method)

1   In a large ovenproof saucepan, heat oil over medium heat. Add onion and cook for 5 minutes, until browned. Add tomatoes, ketchup, brown sugar and lemon juice and stir until thoroughly blended. Bring mixture to a boil. Cover and reduce heat to simmer. Reserve ¼ cup of liquid and set aside.

2   In a large mixing bowl, mix together meat, rice and reserved liquid with a wooden spoon. Add salt and pepper to taste.

3   Place an equal amount (approx. 1 tbsp.) of filling in the middle of each cabbage leaf and roll up, envelope-style.

4   Uncover saucepan and gently lower rolls into sauce. Cover and simmer for about 2 hours.

5   Remove cover from saucepan and place in a preheated 250 degree oven for another 2 hours.

By Esther Mecklinger

To separate the cabbage leaves, put the cabbage in the freezer overnight. The next day, put the cabbage in boiling water for a few minutes. The leaves will separate easily. For an added treat, add a pound of flunken to the pot after cooking the onion.

My Mother's Matzoh and Meat Kugel

This hearty kugel can be cut into squares or pie-shaped wedges, depending on whether you use a rectangular or large round casserole.

Yield: 20 servings.

2 tbsp. oil
3 medium onions, thinly sliced
2 lbs. stewing meat, cut into cubes
Salt and pepper
Water, as needed
½ lb. beef liver, broiled
4 tbsp. oil or parve margarine
8 matzohs, broken into small pieces
Boiling water
10 eggs, beaten
Salt and pepper

1 In a large skillet, heat oil over medium heat. Add onions and cook for 5 minutes. Add stewing meat and sprinkle with salt and pepper. Reduce heat to medium-low; add just enough water to cover bottom of skillet and prevent sticking. Simmer covered for 1½ to 2 hours, until meat is tender, stirring occasionally. Let cool.

2 Pass meat, onions and liver through a meat grinder. Add a little of the gravy from the skillet if the mixture is too dry. This mixture can be refrigerated for 1 day.

3 Place oil or margarine in the bottom of a 3-quart baking dish and place it in a preheated 350 degree oven for about 5 minutes, until hot.

4 Meanwhile, place matzoh pieces in a bowl and pour boiling water over top. Drain immediately and transfer to a large mixing bowl.

5 Add ground meat mixture and eggs to the bowl and mix thoroughly with a wooden spoon. Remove baking dish from the oven and pour mixture into prepared dish. Bake in preheated 350 degree oven for 1 hour, until golden brown.

6 To serve, carefully invert onto a large serving platter. Cut in squares or wedges to serve.

By Lorraine Resnick

The Big Story II

Something's Fishy and Meatless Morsels

Baked Gefilte Fish

It's best to make the fish 1 to 2 days ahead.

Yield: 12 to 16 servings.

⅓ cup oil
4 medium onions, finely chopped
2 medium carrots, grated
3 lbs. chopped fish
4 eggs
2 cups cold water
4 tbsp. matzoh meal
3 to 4 tsp. salt
1 tbsp. pepper
2 tbsp. sugar

1   In a large saucepan, heat oil over medium heat. Add onions and sauté 3 to 5 minutes, or until translucent. Transfer to a mixing bowl. Stir in carrots.

2   Place fish, eggs, water, matzoh meal, salt, pepper and sugar in the bowl of an electric mixer fitted with the paddle. Beat at medium speed for 8 to 10 minutes. Add onions and carrots and beat another 2 minutes.

3   Spoon fish mixture into a Bundt pan that has been sprayed with cooking spray. Pack it down firmly. Bake in preheated 350 degree oven for 1½ hours. A brown crust will form on top during baking. After removing from the oven, peel off the crust.

4   Let cool in the pan for ½ hour. Turn over onto plate and let cool completely before refrigerating.

By Rene Daiter

Baked Salmon with Mustard Crust

Yield: 4 servings.

MUSTARD SAUCE
2 tsp. plus 1 tsp. distilled white vinegar
2 tbsp. sugar
2 tbsp. Dijon mustard
1½ tsp. dry mustard
⅓ cup vegetable or corn oil

Place first 4 ingredients in a blender or the work bowl of a food processor. Blend or process for a few seconds. With the machine running, add the oil and blend until a medium-thick sauce forms. Sauce can be made a day ahead. Cover and refrigerate.

SALMON

4 6-oz. salmon fillets
Salt, pepper and dried thyme
1 recipe Mustard Sauce (above)
4 to 6 tbsp. bread crumbs

1   Place salmon skin-side down in a 9 x 13-inch baking dish that has been sprayed with cooking spray or brushed lightly with oil. Sprinkle salmon with salt, pepper and thyme.

2   Spread 1 tbsp. Mustard Sauce over each fillet, covering completely. Press about 1 to 2 tbsp. bread crumbs on top of each fillet.

3   Bake in preheated 375 degree oven until cooked through and the top is golden brown, about 18 minutes. Transfer to a serving platter and pass remaining sauce separately.

By Heather Gotlieb

Salmon Teriyaki

Yield: 4 servings.

⅛ cup light soy sauce
½ cup teriyaki sauce
1 salmon fillet, about 1½ lbs.
3 tsp. minced fresh garlic
2 tbsp. minced fresh ginger
Lemon wedges, for garnish

1   In a small bowl, whisk together soy and teriyaki sauces.

2   Place salmon fillet skin-side down on a large piece of tinfoil that has been sprayed with cooking spray. Pour soy mixture over salmon. Sprinkle garlic and ginger over top. Seal foil tightly. Marinate in the refrigerator for a few hours or overnight.

3   Preheat barbecue for a few minutes on high. Reduce heat to medium. Cook salmon in foil for 15 to 20 minutes, or until desired degree of doneness. Cover barbecue for the first 10 minutes, then uncover and open up the packet a little bit for the final few minutes of cooking. Arrange salmon on a large serving platter and garnish with lemon wedges.

By Simone Bronfman

Baked Salmon Steaks

Just as easy as it sounds.

Yield: 2 servings.

> 2 6-oz. salmon steaks
> Salt and pepper to taste
> 2 tsp. lemon juice
> 4 tbsp. finely chopped green pepper
> 2 tbsp. cracker crumbs
> 2 2-oz. slices Mozzarella, brick or Cheddar cheese
> 4 slices tomato

1 Place salmon steaks in a baking dish that has been sprayed with cooking spray. Sprinkle with salt and pepper. Drizzle 1 tsp. lemon juice on each steak. Sprinkle 2 tbsp. green pepper on top of each fillet. Sprinkle cracker crumbs over top. Cover each fillet with a slice of cheese and 2 slices of tomato.

2 Bake in preheated 375 degree oven for 30 to 35 minutes.

By Miriam Rose

Hoisin Glazed Salmon

You can substitute sea bass, halibut or tuna for the salmon. Chilled leftovers can be added to rice or salads.

Yield: 4 servings.

> 2 tbsp. hoisin sauce
> 1 tbsp. soy sauce
> 1 tsp. sesame oil
> ¼ tsp. pepper
> 4 6-oz. salmon fillets

1 In a small bowl, whisk together first 4 ingredients.

2 Place fish in a sprayed baking dish. Coat both side of fillets with sauce. Refrigerate 2 to 3 hours.

3 Cook fish about 5 minutes on a preheated barbecue, broiler or electric grill. Alternatively, bake in preheated 425 degree oven, allowing 10 to 12 minutes per inch of thickness.

By Shanea Rakowski

Oriental Salmon

Yield: 4 servings.

    2 tbsp. soy sauce
    1 tbsp. sesame oil
    1 tbsp. minced fresh ginger
    1 small can water chestnuts
    1 carrot, finely julienned
    4 6-oz. salmon fillets
    Salt and pepper to taste

1. In a mixing bowl, whisk together soy sauce, sesame oil and ginger. Add water chestnuts and carrots and stir until combined.

2. Place salmon fillets in a baking dish that has been sprayed with cooking spray. Sprinkle with salt and pepper. Top each fillet with the soy mixture, dividing it evenly. Cover and bake in preheated 375 degree oven for 15 to 20 minutes.

By Marlene Borins

Salmon or Tuna Loaf

Yield: 4 to 6 servings.

    2 cans salmon or tuna, drained
    1 large onion, finely chopped
    3 eggs
    ¾ cup fat-free sour cream or yogurt
    ¼ cup melted butter or margarine
    ¾ cup bread crumbs or matzoh meal

This recipe can also be made in muffin tins. Reduce baking time to 20 to 25 minutes, or until a toothpick inserted comes out clean.

1. Place first 5 ingredients in the work bowl of a food processor and process for 10 seconds, until blended. Add bread crumbs and process another 10 seconds.

2. Transfer to a 9 x 5-inch loaf pan that has been sprayed with cooking spray. Bake in preheated 350 degree oven for 1 hour.

By Faith White

Salmon Tuscany

This recipe is so easy and so delicious. It goes very well with steamed rice and vegetables.

Yield: 4 servings.

4 fresh salmon steaks or fillets
½ cup butter
3 shallots, finely chopped
1½ tsp. chopped fresh tarragon
2 tbsp. soya sauce
1 tsp. lemon juice
Splash of white wine (about ¼ cup)
Freshly ground pepper to taste

1 Line a cookie sheet with tinfoil. Spray with cooking spray. Place salmon pieces along the bottom half of the sheet. (If using fillets, place skin-side down.)

2 In medium skillet, melt butter over medium-low heat. Add shallots and sauté for about 3 minutes. Reduce heat to low and add remaining ingredients. Simmer for a few minutes, stirring with a wooden spoon, until mixture has reduced and thickened slightly.

3 Pour sauce evenly over salmon. Fold top half of foil over salmon. Seal edges of foil together tightly to create a packet.

4 Bake in preheated 375 degree oven for 15 to 20 minutes.

By Wendy Kert

NOTES:

Grilled Halibut with Rosemary Mayonnaise

Yield: 4 servings.

HERB OIL
2 tbsp. mixture of chopped fresh herbs (e.g., thyme, basil and tarragon)
½ cup olive oil

Place herbs in a salad dressing dispenser. Cover with olive oil. Let steep for at least 2 to 3 days.

TOMATO VINAIGRETTE
1 cup tomatoes, peeled, seeded and cut in ½-inch cubes
¼ cup minced fresh herbs (a mixture of basil, parsley, thyme,
    tarragon and fennel)
½ cup lemon juice
2 medium shallots, finely chopped
1 cup olive oil

Place all ingredients in a mixing bowl and stir with a wooden spoon to combine.

ROSEMARY MAYONNAISE
1 tbsp. anchovy paste
2 tbsp. minced fresh rosemary
1 cup mayonnaise

In a small bowl, whisk together all ingredients.

HALIBUT
2 tbsp. mixture of minced fresh thyme and parsley
¼ cup olive oil
4 8-oz. pieces halibut, 1 inch thick
6 medium Japanese eggplants, sliced lengthwise into ¼-inch slices

1 In a small bowl, whisk together thyme, parsley and olive oil. Brush mixture over the halibut.

2 Brush eggplant slices with Herb Oil. Light the barbecue and let it heat up for 10 minutes. Brush the grill with a little oil. Grill the eggplant slices until there are grill marks on each side. Remove and reserve. Grill the halibut 5 to 7 minutes per side.

3 To serve, place halibut and some eggplant slices on individual dinner plates. Spoon some of the Tomato Vinaigrette over the halibut, then garnish with a spoonful of Rosemary Mayonnaise. Place remaining vinaigrette and mayonnaise in separate serving dishes. Serve with grilled halibut and eggplant.

By Debra Verk

Sea Bass with Potatoes

Yield: 2 servings.

> 2 4-oz. sea bass fillets
> 2 tsp. lemon juice
> Salt and pepper to taste
> 2 cups mashed potatoes
> 1 cup steamed bok choy

1   Place fish in a microwavable baking dish. Drizzle lemon juice over top. Sprinkle with salt and pepper. Cover with plastic wrap. Microwave on HIGH power for 3 minutes.

2   To serve, place 1 cup mashed potatoes on each dinner plate and top with ½ cup bok choy. Place sea bass over top.

By Ruth Rosen

Tuna with Raspberry Sauce

Yield: 4 servings.

> 1 cup raspberry preserves
> ½ cup balsamic vinegar
> ⅛ cup soy sauce
> ½ tsp. red pepper flakes
> ½ tsp. cayenne pepper
> 2 tsp. canola oil
> 4 6-oz. pieces yellow fin tuna
> Cracked black pepper

1   In a small saucepan, heat first 5 ingredients over medium-low heat. Reduce heat to simmer. Use a wire whisk to mix raspberry sauce until thoroughly blended.

2   Using two large skillets at the same time, heat 1 tsp. of oil in each one over medium heat. Sprinkle tuna with cracked pepper. Add tuna to skillets and sauté 2 to 3 minutes per side for medium-rare, or until desired degree of doneness.

3   Slice tuna into thin strips and place on a platter. Drizzle the sauce over top.

By Candy Schnier

Tex-Mex Halibut

Yield: 4 servings.

To make Tex-Mex Sea Bass, substitute sea bass fillets for the halibut.

1 tsp. vegetable oil
2 tsp. minced fresh garlic
1 tbsp. jalapeno pepper, finely chopped
1 red pepper, finely chopped
4 4-oz. halibut fillets
¾ tsp. paprika
½ tsp. chili pepper
1 cup dry white wine
¼ cup finely chopped fresh coriander
Pinch of cayenne
¼ tsp. salt

1 In a large skillet, heat oil over medium heat. Add garlic, jalapeno pepper and red pepper and sauté for 3 to 5 minutes, until softened.

2 Place halibut fillets on top of the pepper mixture. Sprinkle paprika and chili pepper over top. Add white wine and bring to a boil. Reduce heat to low, cover and simmer for 6 to 8 minutes.

3 Transfer the fish to a platter. Continue to simmer the sauce until it is reduced to ⅓ cup. Stir in coriander, cayenne and salt. Spoon sauce over the fish.

By Marlene Borins

NOTES:

Rice Noodle and Vegetable Stir Fry

If you want to turn this into a more substantial dish, stir-fry strips of tofu or chicken and add them to this noodle and vegetable mixture. You can add 2 cloves of crushed garlic along with the onion, if desired.

Yield: 4 servings.

1 tbsp. canola oil or cooking spray
1 medium onion, cut in ½-inch dice
2 to 3 cups cut-up vegetables (broccoli, sliced carrots, red and green pepper)
1 can Chinese baby corn, drained
1 can water chestnuts, drained
1 cup chicken or vegetable broth
4 tbsp. light soy sauce
1 package rice noodles
Pepper to taste

1 In a large skillet or wok, heat oil over medium heat (or spray pan with cooking spray). Stir-fry onion for 2 to 3 minutes. Add the rest of the veggies and stir-fry for 1 to 2 minutes. Add chicken broth and soy sauce. Reduce heat to low. Cover and simmer until vegetables are tender-crisp. If you like them softer, cook until desired texture is reached.

2 Meanwhile, soak rice noodles in hot water until soft. Drain and add to vegetable mixture along with pepper. Mix well.

By Marla Shapiro

Vegetarian Chili

Yield: 4 to 6 servings.

1 tbsp. olive oil
1 large onion, finely chopped
2 tsp. minced fresh garlic
3 stalks celery, thinly sliced
1 zucchini, cut in ¼-inch cubes
2 15-oz. cans diced tomatoes
3 tbsp. ketchup
1 tsp. cumin
½ tsp. chili powder
¼ tsp. red pepper flakes
1 19-oz. can red kidney beans, drained

1   In a large saucepan, heat oil over medium heat. Add onion, garlic, celery and zucchini and sauté 5 minutes.

2   Add remaining ingredients and bring to a boil. Reduce heat to low. Cover and simmer for 1 hour, stirring occasionally.

By Fern Sadowski

Tofu Vegetable Stir Fry

Yield: 4 servings.

2 tbsp. vegetable oil
Pinch salt
2 stalks celery, thinly sliced on the diagonal
1 medium onion, thinly sliced
2 green onions, cut in 2-inch pieces
2 tsp. minced fresh garlic
1 15-oz. can baby corn, drained and cut in half
3 medium carrots, thinly sliced on the diagonal
1 head broccoli, cut into florets and steamed
1 14-oz. can straw mushrooms, drained
¼ lb. snow peas, steamed
1 300-gram package extra-firm tofu, cut in strips
1 tbsp. cornstarch
3 tbsp. cold water
2 tbsp. hoisin sauce
2 tbsp. soy sauce
Few drops sesame oil
Salt and pepper

Adding a pinch of salt to the oil prevents it from splattering if it becomes too hot.

1   In a wok, heat oil over medium heat and add a pinch of salt. Add celery, onion, green onions and garlic. Stir-fry for 1 minute, until softened.

2   Add corn, carrots, broccoli, mushrooms and snow peas and stir-fry another minute. Add tofu and stir-fry 1 minute longer.

3   In a small mixing bowl, dissolve cornstarch in water. Whisk in hoisin and soy sauces. Pour into wok and stir-fry an additional minute, until sauce is desired thickness. Sprinkle sesame oil over top. Add salt and pepper to taste.

by May Au

Ricotta Pancakes

Yield: About 2 dozen.

2 cups ricotta cheese
1 cup flour
1 tsp. baking powder
¼ tsp. salt
¾ cup milk or half and half or cream
3 eggs, separated
1 tbsp. honey
½ tsp. vanilla
¼ tsp. grated lemon rind
Butter or margarine for frying

1 Combine cheese, flour, baking powder and salt in a large mixing bowl. Stir until well blended.

2 Add milk, egg yolks, honey, vanilla and lemon rind and stir until blended.

3 Place egg whites in the mixing bowl of an electric mixer fitted with the wire whisk. Beat at medium-high speed until stiff peaks form. Fold into cheese mixture.

4 In a large skillet or griddle, heat 1 tbsp. of butter over medium heat. Drop cheese mixture by rounded spoonfuls into the skillet to form pancakes. Cook about 2 to 3 minutes, until edges of pancakes appear brown and the surface is bubbly. Flip pancakes over and cook about a minute longer.

5 Add butter to skillet as necessary and repeat step 4 until cheese mixture is used up.

By Elise Mecklinger

NOTES:

Blintzes

Yield: 14 to 16 blintzes.

FILLING
1½ lbs. cottage cheese
2 egg yolks, lightly beaten
1 tbsp. melted butter
1 tbsp. sugar

Press cheese through a sieve into a mixing bowl. Add remaining ingredients and stir until well blended.

BATTER
1 cup milk
4 eggs, beaten
1 tsp. salt
1 cup flour

Place milk, eggs and salt in a large mixing bowl and whisk until thoroughly blended. Whisk in flour gradually until smooth.

ASSEMBLY
Melted butter
1 recipe Batter (above)
1 recipe Filling (above)

1   In a 6-inch skillet, heat a little bit of butter over medium-low heat. Add only enough batter to make a very thin pancake, tipping pan from side to side until batter coats bottom of pan. Cook pancake until it blisters. Transfer to a board or a work surface. Repeat with remaining batter.

2   Place 1 rounded tbsp. of filling in the centre of each pancake. Fold over from both sides, then into an envelope shape. Refrigerate until ready to use.

3   Just before serving, in a large skillet, heat a little bit of butter over medium heat. Place blintzes seam-side down in skillet and sauté 2 to 3 minutes per side, until golden brown.

By Suzanne Shuchat

On Rosh Hashanah, I take these blintzes out of the freezer, cover them with a thin coating of butter or margarine and place them in the oven. I set the oven to go on at one o'clock at 325 degrees so that they will be ready for lunch. They take about an hour to bake and come out light and fluffy. Serve with sugar and cinnamon or sour cream and jam.

Crustless Spinach and Mushroom Quiche

The processor makes quick work out of this healthy, flavour-packed quiche from MealLeaniYumm!

Yield: 10 wedges or 3 dozen miniatures.

1 10-oz. package frozen spinach
1 large onion
½ of a red pepper
2 tsp. canola oil
½ lb. mushrooms
2 cloves garlic, minced
2 slices whole wheat bread
1 egg plus 2 egg whites
¾ cup skim milk
½ cup grated low-fat Swiss or Cheddar cheese
1 cup low-fat ricotta or cottage cheese
2 tbsp. grated Parmesan cheese
Salt and pepper to taste
1 tbsp. minced fresh dill

1 Preheat oven to 350 degrees. Spray a 10-inch ceramic quiche dish with nonstick spray (or spray miniature muffin pans very well). Pierce package of spinach with a sharp knife in several places. Place on microsafe plate and microwave on HIGH for 3 to 4 minutes, until defrosted. When cool, remove from package and squeeze dry.

2 In the processor, chop onion and pepper with quick on/offs. In a large nonstick skillet, heat oil on medium-high. Sauté onion and pepper until soft, about 5 minutes. Chop mushrooms with quick on/offs. Add to skillet along with garlic. Sauté 5 minutes longer. Remove from heat; cool slightly.

3 Process bread to make soft crumbs. Add spinach and process until fine. Add egg, egg whites, milk and cheese; mix well. Add sautéed vegetables and mix with quick on/offs. Add seasonings and dill. Spoon mixture into prepared pan(s) and bake at 350 degrees until golden. Bake minis for 18 to 20 minutes or a large quiche for 40 to 45 minutes.

By Norene Gilletz

Fajitas with Goat Cheese and Guacamole

Yield: 4 servings.

Guacamole can also be used as a dip for crudités or pita chips.

GUACAMOLE

2 ripe avocados, halved, pitted and peeled
2 tsp. minced fresh garlic
2 tbsp. lime juice
2 tbsp. prepared salsa
2 tbsp. minced purple onion
1 tbsp. minced fresh cilantro
¼ tsp. chili powder

Place all ingredients in a large mixing bowl. Mix thoroughly with a fork.

FAJITAS

1 tsp. olive oil
1 tsp. minced fresh garlic
½ cup onion, finely chopped
1 small zucchini, cut into matchsticks
¼ tsp. chili powder
4 10-inch flour tortillas
1 cup goat cheese, crumbled
1 cup tomatoes, cut in ¼-inch cubes
1 cup Guacamole (above)

1 In a large skillet, heat oil over medium heat. Add garlic, onion, zucchini and chili powder and sauté 3 to 5 minutes, until golden. Set aside.

2 Lay out tortillas on a work surface. Place ¼ cup of the goat cheese in the middle of each tortilla. Place ¼ cup tomatoes, ¼ cup sautéed vegetables and ¼ cup guacamole in the middle of each tortilla.

3 Roll up each tortilla and wrap in foil. Bake in preheated 350 degree oven for 10 to 15 minutes, or until heated through.

By Elise Mecklinger

Broccoli and Mushroom Calzone

Yield: 4 to 6 servings.

2 tsp. vegetable oil
1 tsp. minced fresh garlic
1½ cups mushrooms, thinly sliced
¼ cup red pepper, finely chopped
1 egg
2 cups frozen broccoli, thawed and drained
¾ cup cottage cheese
⅓ cup grated Parmesan cheese
1 tsp. dried basil
½ tsp. pepper
1 package refrigerated pizza crust

1 In a large skillet, heat oil over medium heat. Add garlic, mushrooms and red pepper and sauté for 3 minutes, until softened. Set aside.

2 In a mixing bowl, lightly beat egg; remove 1 tbsp. and reserve to glaze the dough. Add broccoli, cottage cheese, Parmesan cheese, basil and pepper to remaining egg and mix until well blended. Stir in mushroom mixture.

3 Unroll pizza crust onto a cookie sheet that has been sprayed with cooking spray. Press dough to form a rectangle. Spoon cheese mixture down the centre of the dough. Fold dough over the filling, pinching all edges to seal. Brush with reserved egg.

4 Cut several slits in the top so steam can escape during baking. Bake in preheated 425 degree oven for 15 to 20 minutes, until golden.

By Pamela Ramdeholl

Fondue with Caramelized Onions

Yield: 4 to 6 servings.

1 tbsp. butter

1¼ cups onions, thinly sliced

1 tsp. minced fresh garlic

1 tsp. sugar

Salt and pepper

1½ cups dry white wine

3¼ cups grated Gruyère cheese, packed

2 tbsp. flour

Pinch nutmeg

Salt and pepper

What can you dip in this decadent dish? Besides the obvious sourdough or French bread cubes, try blanched broccoli or cauliflower florets, blanched mushrooms or small steamed new potatoes.

1   In a large skillet, heat butter over medium heat. Add onions and garlic and sauté for 3 minutes, until softened. Reduce heat to low. Sprinkle sugar over onions. Sprinkle with salt and pepper. Continue to sauté slowly for another 15 minutes. Transfer to a bowl.

2   Add wine to the skillet and bring to a boil. Transfer to a medium saucepan and place on medium-low heat. Place cheese in a mixing bowl and toss with flour. Add ½ cup of the onions to the wine. Add cheese mixture by handfuls, stirring until cheese melts before adding more. Sprinkle with nutmeg, salt and pepper.

3   Transfer cheese mixture to fondue pot. Set pot over candle or burner. Top fondue with remaining onions.

By Rona Cappell

NOTES:

Ratatouille

Ratatouille is a robust stew of vegetables which is delicious hot or cold. It makes a delicious side dish or can be topped with melted cheese and baked in the oven until the cheese melts. This also makes an excellent appetizer when served as a dip with crackers, or can be served as a topping over pasta or baked potatoes.

Yield: 8 servings.

1 tbsp. olive oil
1 medium onion, thinly sliced
1 tbsp. minced fresh garlic
1 red pepper, cut in thin strips
1 small eggplant, cut in ½-inch cubes
2 zucchini, sliced in ¼-inch rounds
¼ cup chopped fresh parsley
1 14½-oz. can plum tomatoes, undrained
   (or 2 lbs. plum tomatoes, peeled, seeded and cored)
½ cup tomato paste
¾ cup vegetable broth
1 tsp. honey
1 tsp. chili powder
½ tsp. paprika
½ tsp. marjoram
¼ tsp. pepper
¼ tsp. salt
2 tbsp. chopped fresh parsley

1 In a large saucepan, heat oil over medium heat. Add onion, garlic and red pepper and sauté 5 minutes. Add eggplant, zucchini and 2 tbsp. parsley and cook another 5 minutes. Stir in tomatoes.

2 Meanwhile, in a small bowl, combine tomato paste, broth, honey, chili powder, paprika, marjoram, pepper and salt. Add to saucepan and stir to blend. Reduce heat to low. Simmer 15 to 20 minutes, until vegetables are tender, stirring occasionally. Sprinkle with 2 tbsp. parsley.

By Barbara Kerbel

Sweet Nothings

Best Banana Muffins

Yield: 9 large muffins.

3 large ripe bananas, mashed
¾ cup sugar
1 egg, slightly beaten
⅓ cup melted butter
1½ cups all-purpose flour
1 tsp. baking soda
1 tsp. baking powder
½ tsp. salt

1 Place bananas, sugar and egg in a mixing bowl. Stir until blended. Add melted butter and stir until blended.

2 In another bowl, whisk together flour, baking soda, baking powder and salt. Add dry ingredients to banana mixture and stir just until blended.

3 Pour mixture into 9 large muffins cups that have been sprayed with cooking spray. Bake in preheated 375 degree oven for 20 minutes.

By Anna Koffler

NOTES:

Best-Ever Bran Muffins

Yield: 12 to 15 muffins.

¼ cup oil
½ cup brown sugar
¼ cup molasses
2 eggs
1 cup milk
1½ cups All-Bran cereal
1 cup raisins
1 cup walnuts (optional)
½ cup whole wheat flour
½ cup all-purpose flour
½ tsp. salt
1½ tsp. baking soda

Instead of raisins, you can add 12 chopped dates or 6 coarsely chopped prunes. Instead of walnuts, substitute shelled sunflower seeds. You can also add a spoonful or two of unsalted pumpkin seeds. If desired, sprinkle tops of muffins with sesame seeds before baking.

1 In a large mixing bowl, blend oil and sugar with a wooden spoon. Add molasses and stir until combined.

2 In a small bowl, beat eggs lightly just until mixed. Gradually add milk and beat vigorously with a fork.

3 Slowly add egg mixture to oil mixture. Add bran and raisins and stir with a wooden spoon until combined. Let stand for a few minutes (or cover and refrigerate overnight). Then stir in walnuts, if desired.

4 In a large mixing bowl, mix together flours, salt and baking soda with a wire whisk. Add to bran mixture and stir just until combined.

5 Pour into muffin tins that have been lined with paper liners. Fill tins ⅔ full. Bake about 20 minutes in preheated 400 degree oven or until tops of muffins spring back when lightly touched. Turn out of pan immediately.

By Judy Slan

Cranberry Apple Muffins

Yield: 1 dozen muffins.

2 cups flour
¾ cup sugar
1 tsp. baking soda
1 tsp. baking powder
Pinch salt
3 tbsp. oil
1 egg
¼ cup lemon juice
½ cup orange juice
1 cup peeled, cored and chopped apple
½ cup cranberries

1   In a large bowl, whisk together flour, sugar, baking soda, baking powder and salt. In another bowl, whisk together oil, egg and juices. Stir oil mixture into dry ingredients and mix just until blended.

2   Put half the batter into 12 muffin tins that have been sprayed with cooking spray. Divide half of apples and cranberries among the muffins. Add remaining batter; top with remaining apples and cranberries. Bake in preheated 375 degree oven for 20 minutes.

By Dr. Marvin Gelkopf

Butterscotch Bars

Yield: 15 bars.

½ cup sugar
½ cup packed brown sugar
¼ cup butter or margarine, softened
2 large egg whites
1 tsp. vanilla
1¼ cups all-purpose flour
½ tsp. baking powder
¼ tsp. salt
½ cup butterscotch morsels

1 Place sugars and butter in a large mixing bowl. Using an electric mixer, beat at medium speed until well blended, about 4 minutes. Add egg whites and vanilla and beat well.

2 In another mixing bowl, combine flour, baking powder and salt with a wire whisk. Add flour mixture to batter and beat at low speed just until blended.

3 Spread batter evenly in an 8 x 8-inch baking pan that has been sprayed with cooking spray. Sprinkle evenly with butterscotch morsels. Bake in preheated 350 degree oven for 28 minutes, or until a wooden pick inserted in centre comes out clean. Cool the pan on a wire rack. Cut into bars.

By Dr. Marvin Gelkopf

Chocolate Chip Bars

Yield: 15 bars.

> 1 cup brown sugar
> 1 cup butter, softened
> 1 egg
> 1 tbsp. vanilla
> 2 cups all-purpose flour
> ½ tsp. baking soda
> 2 cups semi-sweet chocolate chips

1 Place sugar and butter in the bowl of an electric mixer fitted with the paddle. Beat at medium speed until blended. Add egg and vanilla and continue to beat until smooth. Reduce to low speed and add flour and baking soda, mixing just until blended. Stir in chocolate chips with a wooden spoon.

2 Pour mixture into an 8 x 8-inch glass baking pan that has been sprayed with cooking spray. Bake in preheated 300 degree oven for 35 to 45 minutes. Let cool. Cut into bar-shaped pieces.

By Noni Plener

Easy Lemon Squares

Yield: 32 squares.

CRUST
½ cup sugar
6 tbsp. margarine (¾ of a stick), softened
2 cups all-purpose flour

1 Place sugar and margarine in a mixing bowl. Beat with an electric mixer until well-creamed. Gradually add flour and mix on low speed until mixture resembles fine crumbs.

2 Press into the bottom of a 9 x 13-inch baking pan. Bake in preheated 350 degree oven for 15 minutes, until golden. Cool on a wire rack.

TOPPING
3 large eggs and 3 egg whites
1½ cups sugar
4 tsp. grated lemon rind
⅔ cup fresh lemon juice
6 tbsp. all-purpose flour
1 tsp. baking powder
¼ tsp. salt
4 tsp. powdered sugar

1 Place eggs and egg whites in a large mixing bowl. Beat with electric mixer at medium speed until foamy. Add sugar, lemon rind, juice, flour, baking powder and salt. Beat until well blended.

2 Pour mixture over partially baked crust. Bake at 350 degrees for 20 to 25 minutes, or until golden and set. Cool on wire rack. Sift powdered sugar evenly over top. Cut into squares.

By Dr. Marvin Gelkopf

Fudge Peanut Butter Cup Brownies

Yield: 32 brownies.

MILK CHOCOLATE SAUCE
8 oz. milk chocolate
¼ cup boiling water
½ tsp. vanilla

Place chocolate in a bowl. Pour boiling water over top and stir until melted. Stir in vanilla.

BROWNIES
12 ounces semi-sweet chocolate, coarsely chopped
12 tbsp. (1½ sticks) unsalted butter, cut up
6 eggs
1¾ cups sugar
2 tsp. vanilla
1½ cups all-purpose flour
½ tsp. salt
24 miniature chocolate-covered peanut butter cups

For a special treat, sprinkle chopped roasted peanuts over the top. Otherwise, simply invert the brownies and let them cool. Then cut into squares and top with sauce

1   In a microwavable bowl, combine chocolate and butter. Microwave uncovered on HIGH power for 2 to 3 minutes, until melted, stirring 2 or 3 times. Set aside. (Or melt butter and chocolate together in the top of a double boiler. Stir to combine.)

2   Place eggs in the mixing bowl of an electric mixer fitted with the wire whisk. Beat eggs until foamy, about 2 minutes. Add sugar and beat 2 minutes longer, or until well blended. Blend in chocolate mixture and vanilla. Gradually add flour and salt and mix just until blended.

3   Pour half the batter into 9 x 13-inch baking pan that has been lined with parchment paper or sprayed with cooking spray. Arrange peanut butter cups evenly over batter. Pour remaining batter over peanut butter cups.

4   Bake in a preheated 350 degree oven for 25 to 30 minutes. Cool brownies completely. Spread sauce over top. Cut into squares.

By Shanea Rakowski

Cake-Like Brownies

Yield: 16 brownies.

¼ lb. butter
2 squares unsweetened chocolate
2 eggs
1 cup sugar
1 tsp. vanilla
¾ cup flour
2 tsp. baking powder
½ cup milk

1 Place butter and chocolate in a glass bowl. Microwave on HIGH power for 2 to 3 minutes, until melted, stirring 2 or 3 times. Cool.

2 Place eggs and sugar in a mixing bowl. With an electric mixer, beat until fluffy. Add vanilla. Fold in chocolate mixture and mix thoroughly.

3 In another bowl, whisk together flour and baking powder. Add milk alternately with dry ingredients to batter and mix until blended. Pour into an 8 x 8-inch baking pan that has been sprayed with cooking spray. Bake in preheated 350 degree oven for 30 minutes. When cool, cut into squares.

By Lesley Campbell

Noreen's Brownies

Yield: 32 brownies.

4 squares unsweetened chocolate, melted and cooled
1 cup chocolate chips, melted and cooled
1 cup butter, melted and cooled
4 eggs
2 cups sugar
2 tsp. vanilla
1 cup flour
½ tsp. salt
1 tsp. baking powder
2 cups mini marshmallows

1 In a large bowl, whisk together melted chocolate, chocolate chips and butter. Place eggs, sugar and vanilla in a large mixing bowl. With an electric mixer, beat until combined. Add chocolate mixture and beat until blended.

2 In a large bowl, whisk together flour, salt and baking powder. Gradually stir into batter. Stir in marshmallows. Pour into 9 x 13-inch baking pan that has been sprayed with cooking spray. Spread evenly in pan. Bake in preheated 350 degree oven for 40 to 45 minutes.

By Noreen Brown

Dave's Chocolate Brownies

Yield: 18 brownies.

½ cup butter or low-fat margarine
2 squares unsweetened chocolate
1 cup sugar
½ cup all-purpose flour
½ tsp. baking powder
2 eggs
1 tsp. vanilla
1 can (14-oz.) low-fat sweetened condensed milk
1 cup graham cracker crumbs
¾ cup chocolate chips

My absolutely favourite recipe! When my son was young, these used to be called Davey's Chocolate Brownies, but he grew up, so I had to change the name of the recipe!

1 In a microwavable bowl, combine butter and chocolate. Microwave uncovered on HIGH for 2 to 3 minutes, or until mixture has melted, stirring 2 or 3 times. Set aside. (Or melt butter and chocolate together in the top part of a double boiler. Stir to combine.)

2 Place sugar, flour and baking powder in the work bowl of a food processor. Process for 10 seconds. While the machine is running, add eggs, vanilla and chocolate mixture and process until blended, about 10 seconds.

3 Add condensed milk, graham cracker crumbs and chocolate chips to the work bowl. Process for 20 seconds.

4 Pour into a 7 x 11-inch baking dish that has been sprayed with cooking spray. Bake in preheated 350 degree oven for 35 minutes, or until a crust has formed on top. Cool and cut into squares.

By Elise Mecklinger

Harriette from Halifax's Brownies

If you double the brownie recipe, it is not necessary to double the icing recipe.

Yield: 16 brownies.

½ cup butter or margarine, softened

1 cup sugar

2 eggs

2 squares unsweetened chocolate

1 tsp. vanilla

¾ cup flour

½ tsp. baking powder

¼ tsp. salt

½ package marshmallows, cut in half

1. Place butter and sugar in a large mixing bowl. Use an electric mixer to beat until combined. Add eggs one at a time and beat until blended.

2. Place chocolate in a glass bowl. Microwave on MEDIUM power for 2 to 3 minutes, until melted, stirring 2 or 3 times. Add to butter mixture and beat until smooth. Blend in vanilla.

3. In another bowl, whisk together flour, baking powder and salt. Add to butter mixture, mixing just until blended. Pour into a greased and floured 8 or 9-inch square baking pan.

4. Bake in preheated 350 degree oven for 20 to 25 minutes, until firm. Remove from oven. While still hot, cover with a layer of marshmallows. Put back in the oven for 5 to 10 minutes. Watch carefully to avoid burning.

ICING

3 tbsp. butter, melted

2 squares unsweetened chocolate, melted

2 cups icing sugar

¼ cup milk

½ tsp. vanilla

1. Combine butter and chocolate and stir until blended. Place icing sugar, milk and vanilla in a mixing bowl. With an electric mixer, beat until smooth.

2. Add chocolate mixture and stir until blended. Let stand until firm. Spread over cooled brownies.

By Harriette Laing

Mount Sinai Mandelbroit

Yield: About 4 dozen.

These are so delicious!

3 large eggs
1 cup oil
1 cup sugar
1 tsp. vanilla
2 cups flour
2 cups corn flakes
1 tsp. baking powder
½ to ¾ cup chocolate chips

1 In a large mixing bowl, whisk together eggs, oil, sugar and vanilla. In another bowl, combine flour, corn flakes, baking powder and chocolate chips. Add dry ingredients to batter and stir until combined.

2 Divide mixture into 4 equal logs. Spray 2 cookie sheets with cooking spray. Place 2 logs on each cookie sheet. Bake in preheated 350 degree oven for 20 to 25 minutes.

3 Remove from oven. Cut each log diagonally into 1-inch slices. Place slices on their sides and bake about 20 minutes longer, or until brown on all sides.

By Hinda Silber

NOTES:

Bubby's Mandelbroit

Yield: About 5 dozen.

3 eggs
1 cup oil
1 tsp. vanilla
1 cup sugar
4 cups flour (reserve 1 cup for kneading the dough)
1½ tsp. baking powder
1 cup toasted almonds, coarsely chopped

1 In a large mixing bowl, whisk together eggs, oil and vanilla. Add sugar, 3 cups of the flour and baking powder. Stir with a wooden spoon until thoroughly blended.

2 On a wooden board, knead mixture with the reserved cup of flour until mixture is no longer sticky.

3 Separate dough into 3 sections and roll into logs approximately 1 inch thick. Place logs on a cookie sheet that has been lined with parchment paper. Bake in preheated 350 degree oven for 25 to 30 minutes. Remove from oven and let cool.

4 Reduce heat to 325 degrees. Cut each log diagonally into 1-inch slices. Place slices on their sides and bake 10 to 12 minutes longer.

By Shari Borenstein

Chocolate Chip Mandelbroit

Yield: About 4 dozen.

3 eggs
¾ cup sugar
1 cup oil
1½ tsp. vanilla
2½ cups flour
3 tsp. baking powder
2 cups chocolate chips
1 cup sliced blanched almonds (optional)

1   In a large mixing bowl, whisk together eggs, sugar, oil and vanilla. Stir in flour, baking powder, chocolate chips and almonds (if using), until blended. Put mixture in refrigerator for at least ½ hour.

2   Shape batter into 3 equal logs and place on cookie sheets that have been sprayed with cooking spray. Bake in preheated 350 degree oven for 25 minutes.

3   Remove from oven. Cut each log diagonally into 1-inch slices. Place slices on their sides and bake about 20 minutes longer, or until brown on all sides.

By Faith White

Biscotti

Yield: About 4 dozen biscotti.

2 eggs
1 cup sugar
1 cup oil
1 tsp. vanilla
2 cups all-purpose flour
½ tsp. salt
2 tsp. baking powder
2 cups Rice Krispies
½ lb. chopped almonds
1 cup chocolate chips, white chocolate chips or dried cranberries
1 tbsp. cinnamon mixed with 3 tbsp. sugar

1   Place eggs and sugar in a large mixing bowl. Using an electric mixer, beat on medium speed until blended. Add oil and vanilla and beat until blended.

2   In a small mixing bowl, whisk together flour, salt and baking powder. Gradually add dry ingredients to egg mixture. Add Rice Krispies, almonds and chocolate chips or cranberries to the batter. The batter will be loose.

3   Divide the batter into 2 equal parts. Form into logs and place on a greased cookie sheet. Bake in preheated 325 degree oven for 30 minutes.

4   Slice logs crosswise into 1-inch slices. Lay slices flat on cookie sheet. Sprinkle with cinnamon/sugar mixture. Bake another 10 minutes, until brown.

By Linda Friedlich

Dara's Triple Delight

Yield: About 36 cookies.

1 cup unsalted butter, softened
¾ cup sugar
¾ cup brown sugar, packed
2 eggs
1 tsp. vanilla
2½ cups flour
1 tsp. baking soda
1 cup Skor toffee bits
¼ cup semi-sweet chocolate chips
¼ cup milk chocolate chips

1   Place butter and sugars in a large mixing bowl. Using an electric mixer, beat on medium speed until creamy. Add eggs and vanilla and beat until combined.

2   In another bowl, whisk together flour and baking soda. Add toffee bits and chocolate chips to batter and stir until combined.

3   Drop batter by heaping teaspoonfuls onto greased baking sheets. Bake in preheated 350 degree oven for 12 to 14 minutes, or until cookies flatten and edges are slightly browned. Cool on racks.

By Dara Rakowski

Malco's Night and Day Cookies

These two-toned cookies are scrumptious!

Yield: About 6 dozen cookies.

1 cup butter, softened
¾ cup sugar
¾ cup brown sugar
2 eggs
2 tsp. vanilla
2 cups all-purpose flour
½ tsp. baking soda
2 cups chocolate chips
½ cup cocoa

1   Place butter and sugars in a large mixing bowl. With an electric mixer, beat until creamy. Add eggs and vanilla and beat until blended.

2   In another bowl, whisk together flour and baking soda. Stir in chocolate chips. Add to butter mixture. Mix just until combined.

3   Divide the mixture into 2 equal parts. Add cocoa to one part and mix well. Refrigerate for about ½ hour so dough will be easier to handle.

4   Drop ½ tsp. of each mixture onto a cookie sheet side by side, overlapping slightly. Cookies should be 2 inches apart as they will spread during baking. Bake in preheated 375 degree oven for 8 to 9 minutes.

By Liora Yakobowicz

Chocolate Chip Crunch Cookies

Yield: About 18 cookies.

¼ cup unsalted butter, softened
⅓ cup brown sugar
1 egg yolk
2 tsp. water
¼ tsp. vanilla
½ cup flour
¼ tsp. baking powder
¼ tsp. salt
1 cup chocolate chips
½ cup toasted rice cereal (e.g., Rice Krispies)

1   Place butter and sugar in the mixing bowl of an electric mixer fitted with the paddle. Beat until light and fluffy. Add egg yolk, water and vanilla and beat until blended.

2   Place flour, baking powder and salt in another bowl. Stir with a wire whisk until well combined. Gradually add to butter mixture and beat on low speed until well blended. Stir in chocolate chips and rice cereal.

3   Drop batter from a tablespoon onto a cookie sheet that has been lined with parchment paper or sprayed with cooking spray. Cookies should be 2 inches apart. Bake in preheated 350 degree oven for 8 to 10 minutes, or until golden. Transfer to a rack to cool.

By Shanea Rakowski

Faith's Best-Ever Oatmeal Cookies

Yield: About 6 dozen cookies.

3 cups flour
1 tbsp. baking powder
1 tbsp. baking soda
1 tbsp. cinnamon
1 tsp. salt
1½ cups butter, at room temperature
1 cup sugar
1 cup brown sugar
3 eggs
1 tbsp. vanilla
3 cups semi-sweet chocolate chips
3 cups rolled oats
3 cups sweetened flaked coconut
2 cups chopped pecans
1 cup craisins (optional)

1   In a large mixing bowl, combine flour, baking powder, soda, cinnamon and salt.

2   Place butter in the mixing bowl of an electric mixer fitted with the paddle. Beat on medium speed until smooth, about 1 minute. Gradually add sugars and beat an additional 2 minutes.

3   Add eggs one at a time, beating well after each addition. Beat in vanilla.

4   Stir in flour mixture just until combined. Add chocolate chips, rolled oats, coconut, pecans and craisins. Mix well.

5   For each cookie, drop 1 heaping tablespoon dough onto an ungreased cookie sheet about 3 inches apart. Bake in preheated 350 degree oven for 14 to 17 minutes, until edges are lightly browned. Rotate baking sheets halfway through baking. Remove cookies onto a rack to cool.

By Faith White

Chocolate Chip Meringues

Yield: About 3 dozen cookies.

3 egg whites
½ tsp. salt
¾ cup sugar
1 tsp. vanilla
3 cups corn flakes
¾ cup chocolate chips

1 Place egg whites and salt in a mixing bowl. Using an electric mixer, beat until soft peaks form. Gradually beat in sugar and vanilla until stiff peaks form. Fold in corn flakes and chocolate chips.

2 Drop by heaping teaspoonfuls onto greased cookie sheets. Bake in preheated 350 degree oven for 15 to 18 minutes. Cool slightly before removing from pans.

By Suzanne Shuchat

Bake While You Sleep Meringues

Yield: About 30 cookies.

2 egg whites
Pinch of salt
⅔ cup sugar
½ tsp. vanilla
1 cup chocolate chips
1 cup chopped nuts (optional)

These are wonderful for Passover. Kids love them!

1 Preheat oven to 350 degrees.

2 Place egg whites and salt in the bowl of an electric mixer fitted with the wire whisk. Beat at medium speed until soft peaks form. Gradually beat in sugar and vanilla and continue to beat until stiff peaks form. Fold in chocolate chips and nuts (if using).

3 Drop by teaspoonfuls onto a lightly greased cookie sheet. Place in oven and turn oven off. Go to bed. These cookies will bake while you sleep.

By Ellin Kert

Malco's Meringue Triangles

Yield: About 2½ to 3 dozen. These should be stored in the refrigerator.

MERINGUES
2 cups hazelnuts
2 cups egg whites
Pinch salt
Pinch cream of tartar
1 cup sugar

1 Place hazelnuts on a cookie sheet and toast in preheated 325 degree oven for 10 to 15 minutes. Let cool. Wrap nuts in a kitchen towel and rub until skins comes off. Place nuts in work bowl of food processor and pulse until finely ground.

2 Place eggs whites, salt and cream of tartar in a large mixing bowl. Using an electric mixer, beat until fluffy. Gradually add sugar 1 tbsp. at a time and beat until stiff peaks form, but meringue is not too dry. Fold in hazelnuts with a rubber spatula.

3 Line two 12 x 18-inch baking sheets with parchment or waxed paper. Divide meringue mixture in half. Spread half of meringue mixture on each baking sheet. Bake in preheated 400 degree oven for 10 minutes. Reduce oven temperature to 250 degrees and bake for 2 hours. Do NOT open the door until oven has completely cooled down.

GANACHE
2 cups whipping cream
1¾ cups chocolate chips

In a medium saucepan, heat whipping cream over medium heat until boiling. Remove from heat. Add chocolate chips, stirring until completely melted. To cool down the ganache mixture quickly, place it in the refrigerator.

ASSEMBLY

1 Carefully remove parchment paper from the two sheets of meringue. Spread ganache evenly over the top of each meringue. Refrigerate overnight.

2 Slice each meringue sheet in half lengthwise. Put on top of one another to create a 4-decker layer. Slice into small triangles and arrange on a plate.

By Liora Yakubowicz

Chocolate Almond Triangles

Yield: 1 dozen pastries.

To defrost the phyllo dough, place the unopened package in the refrigerator for 2 days

ALMOND FILLING

1 tsp. grated lemon zest
1 tbsp. lemon juice
6 oz. cream cheese, softened
½ lb. marzipan or almond paste
2 tbsp. flour

Place all ingredients in the work bowl of a food processor fitted with the steel blade. Pulse on and off until all ingredients are combined. Transfer to a small mixing bowl. Cover and refrigerate at least 1 hour or overnight.

ASSEMBLY

8 sheets phyllo dough
½ cup butter, melted and slightly cooled
1 recipe Almond Filling (above)
2 oz. bittersweet chocolate (e.g., Lindt), cut into 12 chunks

1   Unfold phyllo dough and lay it out on a work surface. Place waxed paper over phyllo, then cover with a damp dishtowel to prevent it from drying out.

2   Remove one sheet of phyllo and keep the rest covered. Brush lightly with melted butter. Place a second sheet of phyllo over top and brush with butter.

3   Cut dough lengthwise into 3 strips, each about 4½ inches wide. Place a generous tablespoon of filling 1 inch from the bottom of each strip. Place a small chunk of chocolate in the middle of the filling. Fold dough upwards once so that filling is covered. Then fold into a triangle shape, just like you would fold a flag. Continue folding upwards and from side to side until the strip is completely folded.

4   Repeat steps 2 and 3 until all phyllo is used.

5   Place finished pastry triangles seam-side down on a baking sheet that has been brushed with melted butter. Brush tops of pastries with remaining butter.

6   Bake in preheated 375 degree oven for about 20 minutes, until golden brown. Serve warm or at room temperature.

By Debra Verk

Susanah's Scrunchies

Yield: 8 dozen small cookies.

1 cup butter, softened
1 ¼ cup brown sugar
2 tbsp. pure maple syrup
1 egg
1 cup rolled oats
1 cup shredded coconut
½ cup lightly toasted peanuts, quartered
½ cup chocolate chips
2 cups plus 2 tbsp. pastry flour
2 tsp. baking powder
¼ tsp. baking soda
½ tsp. salt

1   Place butter, brown sugar, maple syrup and egg in a large mixing bowl. With an electric mixer, beat at low speed until blended. Add oats, coconut, peanuts and chocolate chips. Stir until combined. Cover and refrigerate overnight.

2   In a mixing bowl, whisk together flour, baking powder, baking soda and salt. Add dry ingredients to the butter mixture and stir until thoroughly blended.

3   Drop by rounded teaspoonfuls onto greased cookie sheets. Make sure that cookies are not too close together as they will spread during baking. Bake in preheated 375 degree oven for about 10 minutes, until golden brown. Cool thoroughly.

By Pearl Stone

Toffee Fingers

Yield: About 5 dozen.

27 to 30 single graham wafers
1 ¼ cups butter, melted
1 cup sugar
½ cup slivered almonds
Sesame seeds

1 Line a cookie sheet with tinfoil. Lay out wafers on the cookie sheet so that sides of wafers are touching each other. In a small bowl, whisk together butter and sugar. Stir in almonds. Spread mixture evenly over wafers. Sprinkle with sesame seeds.

2 Bake in preheated 350 degree oven for 9 minutes, until bubbly. Cut into fingers while warm. Store in the refrigerator.

By Eleanor Long

Microwave Peanut Brittle

Yield: About 1 lb.

1 cup sugar
⅓ cup corn syrup
1 cup roasted salted peanuts
1 tsp. butter
1 tsp. vanilla
1 tsp. baking soda

To make Almond Brittle, substitute almonds for the peanuts and almond extract for the vanilla.

1 In a large microwavable bowl that is heat-resistant, combine sugar and corn syrup. Microwave uncovered on HIGH power for 4 minutes.

2 Stir in peanuts with a wooden spoon. Microwave an additional 3 minutes. Add butter and vanilla and stir until blended. Microwave another 1 to 2 minutes. The peanuts will be light brown and the syrup will be very hot

3 With a wooden spoon, stir in baking soda until the mixture is light and foamy.

4 Using a spatula, spread the mixture onto a cookie sheet that has been greased with butter or sprayed with cooking spray. Cool for 30 minutes to 1 hour. When cool, break into small pieces. Store in an airtight container.

By Shanea Rakowski

Peanut Crisp

No time to frost these squares? They taste great even without frosting.

Yield: 16 squares.

SQUARES
½ cup brown sugar
½ cup corn syrup
¾ cup crunchy peanut butter
1 tsp. vanilla
3 cups Rice Krispies cereal

1   In the top of a double boiler, combine sugar and corn syrup. Place over boiling water and bring mixture to a boil. Let boil for 2 to 3 minutes. Remove the pot from the heat, but leave the top of the double boiler over the hot water.

2   Add peanut butter and vanilla and stir until blended. Add cereal and coat well. Pour into greased 9 x 9-inch baking pan.

ICING
⅛ cup butter
½ cup brown sugar
⅛ cup milk
½ cup icing sugar

1   In a small saucepan, heat butter, sugar and milk over medium heat. Bring mixture to a boil and cook until it forms a thread when dropped from the edge of a spoon (238 to 240 degrees on a candy thermometer). Let mixture cool. Add icing sugar and stir until well blended.

2   Spread icing over Rice Krispies mixture. Cut in squares when ready to serve.

By Toni Bailie

Easy Almond Roca

If desired, store these little treats between layers of wax paper in the refrigerator. They also freeze well.

Yield: 40 pieces.

2 sleeves soda crackers (about 40)
1 cup soft margarine (not calorie-reduced)
1 cup brown sugar, lightly packed
1 cup semi-sweet chocolate chips
1 cup sliced almonds

1   Line a jelly roll pan with wax paper, making sure that paper extends up sides of pan. Place crackers in a single layer, with their sides touching, until the bottom of the pan is covered from edge to edge. Make sure that there is no overlapping of crackers. Set aside.

2   In a medium saucepan, heat margarine over medium heat. Add sugar and combine with a wire whisk. Bring to a slow rolling boil and let boil for 3 minutes without stirring.

3   Pour butterscotch mixture evenly over the crackers and spread evenly, being careful not to overlap the crackers. Bake in preheated 350 degree oven for 10 minutes.

4   Meanwhile, melt chocolate chips in the top of a double boiler (microwave not recommended for this) until thin enough to drizzle.

5   Remove pan from oven and place on cooling rack. Drizzle melted chocolate evenly over crackers. Sprinkle with almonds and let stand for 10 minutes. Separate the crackers and place them on a new layer of waxed paper. Let cool completely.

By Sherry Coote

Sugar-Free Baked Apples

Yield: 12 servings.

12 large cooking apples (McIntosh, Spy, Granny Smith)
24 tbsp. brown Sugar Twin
12 tsp. cinnamon
1 can diet ginger ale

1   Wash apples well. Cut a lid off the top of each apple; reserve lids. Core apples, making sure not to puncture the bottoms.

2   Place apples in a 9 x 13-inch glass baking dish that has been sprayed with cooking spray. Fill empty in each apple and fill with 2 tbsp. sugar substitute.

3   Sprinkle each apple with 1 tsp. cinnamon. Pour ginger ale into baking dish around the apples. Replace lids on apples. Bake in preheated 350 degree oven for 30 minutes, or until soft. Serve hot or cold.

By May Cappell

Great Temptations

World's Best Banana Bread

Yield: 1 loaf.

1 cup sugar
2 eggs
½ cup butter, softened
2 to 3 ripe bananas
1¼ cups flour
1 tsp. baking soda
⅓ cup nuts or chocolate chips (optional)

1 Place sugar, eggs, butter and bananas in the work bowl of a food processor fitted with the steel blade. Process for about 20 seconds, until well blended.

2 Add flour and baking soda. Using on/off turns, process until just blended. Add nuts or chocolate chips, if desired.

3 Pour into a 9 x 5-inch loaf pan that has been sprayed with cooking spray. Bake in pre-heated 350 degree oven for 55 to 60 minutes. Remove from pan and cool on rack.

By Barbara Bregman

I make this cake at least once a week. It's fabulous for breakfast or a snack.

Daniel's Banana Bread

Yield: 1 loaf.

1¼ cups flour
1 tsp. baking powder
2 eggs, beaten
½ cup oil
1 cup sugar
2 ripe bananas, mashed

1 In a mixing bowl, whisk together flour and baking powder. In another mixing bowl, whisk together eggs, oil and sugar. Add to flour mixture and stir until blended. Add bananas and stir until blended.

2 Pour into a 9 x 5-inch loaf pan that has been sprayed with cooking spray. Bake in preheated 350 degree oven for 1 hour.

By Wendy Kert

Kids love to make this one – it's so very, very simple. If desired, add ½ cup chocolate chips or walnuts.

Yummy Yogurt Banana Bread

This recipe is a healthy treat that kids love. To reduce the fat content, use nonfat yogurt, 1 egg and 2 egg whites. Substitute dried fruit, nuts or raisins for the chocolate chips.

Yield: 1 loaf.

¼ cup canola oil
¾ cup sugar
2 eggs (or 1 egg and 2 egg whites)
1 tsp. vanilla
¾ cup vanilla yogurt
3 ripe bananas
1 tsp. baking soda
1 tsp. baking powder
1 cup whole wheat flour
1 cup all-purpose flour
1 tsp. cinnamon
¾ cup chocolate chips

1 Place oil and sugar in the work bowl of a food processor fitted with the steel blade. Process for 1 minute. Add eggs and vanilla and process another minute. Add yogurt and bananas and process another 2 minutes, until smooth. Scrape down sides of bowl as necessary.

2 In a large mixing bowl, whisk together baking soda, baking powder, flours and cinnamon. Add dry ingredients to processor bowl and process with on/off turns just until combined. Stir in chocolate chips.

3 Pour into 9 x 5-inch loaf pan that has been sprayed with cooking spray. Bake in preheated 325 degree oven for 55 minutes.

By Linda Waks

NOTES:

Gluten-Free Banana Loaf

Yield: 1 loaf.

GLUTEN-FREE FLOUR MIX
2 cups white rice flour
⅔ cup potato starch
⅓ cup tapioca starch

Xanthan gum is used in gluten-free baked goods as a substitute for gluten. It is available in health food stores.

Sift ingredients together twice. Store in airtight container. This makes 3 cups gluten-free flour mix.

LOAF
1 cup ripe mashed bananas
1 tsp. baking soda
½ cup low-fat yogurt
¼ cup vegetable oil
¾ cup brown sugar
1 egg
1 tsp. vanilla
1½ cups Gluten-Free Flour Mix (above)
1 tsp. xanthan gum
1 tsp. baking powder
Pinch salt

1. In a small bowl, combine bananas, baking soda and yogurt. Let stand for a few minutes.

2. In a medium bowl, combine oil, brown sugar, egg and vanilla. Mix until well blended.

3. In a large mixing bowl, sift together Gluten-Free Flour Mix, xanthan gum, baking powder, and salt three times.

4. Add banana mixture to oil mixture and stir with a fork until combined. Add to dry ingredients and stir until blended.

5. Pour into a lightly greased 9 x 5-inch loaf pan. Bake in preheated 350 degree oven for 50 minutes.

By Mimi Green

It Doesn't Last Cake

This is a very dense cake that is full of flavour but doesn't taste too sweet. It comes out perfectly every time!

Yield: 12 to 15 servings.

3 cups flour

3 cups sugar

2 tsp. baking soda

1 tsp. salt

1 tsp. cinnamon

1⅓ cups vegetable oil

1½ tsp. vanilla

1 cup crushed pineapple (with the juice)

2 cups mashed bananas

1 cup chopped pecans (optional)

1   Place flour, sugar, baking soda, salt and cinnamon in a large mixing bowl. Stir with a wooden spoon until well combined.

2   Make a well in the centre and add oil, vanilla, pineapple and bananas. Gradually mix in the dry ingredients with a wooden spoon until thoroughly blended. Add nuts if desired.

3   Pour into a 10-inch Bundt pan that has been sprayed with cooking spray. Bake in pre-heated 350 degree oven for 1¼ hours, or until a toothpick inserted in cake comes out clean.

By Barbara Bregman

Eric's Banana Chocolate Chip Cake

Yield: 9 servings.

½ cup butter, softened

1¼ cups sugar

2 eggs

1 tsp. vanilla

1 tsp. baking soda

¼ cup sour cream

1½ cups flour

1 tsp. baking powder

1 cup mashed ripe bananas

½ cup milk chocolate chips

1. Place butter, sugar, eggs and vanilla in a mixing bowl. Using an electric mixer, beat until light and fluffy. Dissolve baking soda in sour cream. Add to batter.

2. In another bowl, whisk together flour and baking powder. Add mashed bananas to batter alternately with dry ingredients and mix well. Add chocolate chips and stir until blended.

3. Pour batter into a 9 x 9-inch baking pan that has been sprayed with cooking spray. Bake in preheated 350 degree oven for 40 to 45 minutes.

By Rona Cappell

Chocolate Chip Bundt Cake

Yield: 16 servings.

2 tsp. all-purpose flour
1 cup fat-free sour cream
¾ cup plus 1 tbsp. warm water
3 tbsp. vegetable oil
4 tsp. instant coffee granules
1 8-oz. carton egg substitute
1 package (18 oz.) devil's food cake mix (without pudding in the mix)
1 package (4 oz.) chocolate instant pudding mix
½ cup semi-sweet chocolate chips
1 tbsp. powdered sugar

1. Coat a 12-cup Bundt pan with cooking spray, then dust it with flour. Set aside.

2. In a large mixing bowl, combine sour cream, water, oil, coffee, egg substitute, cake mix and pudding mix. Using an electric mixer, beat mixture for 3 minutes on medium speed. Add chocolate chips and beat the mixture for 30 seconds.

3. Spoon the batter into prepared pan. Bake in a preheated 350 degree oven for 1 hour, until a wooden pick inserted in the centre comes out clean.

4. Cool cake in pan 10 minutes on a wire rack. Invert cake onto rack and cool completely. Sprinkle cake with powdered sugar.

By Dr. Marvin Gelkopf

Max's Favourite Cake

This unusual chocolate chip coffee cake is made with ricotta cheese. I'm sure it will become a favourite of yours!

Yield: 12 servings.

1 cup ricotta cheese

⅓ cup butter, softened

1¼ cups sugar

2 eggs

2 tsp. vanilla

1½ cups flour

2 tsp. baking powder

½ tsp. baking soda

¾ cup sour cream

½ cup milk chocolate chips

½ cup brown sugar

3 tsp. cocoa

½ tsp. cinnamon

1. Place ricotta cheese, butter and sugar in a large mixing bowl. With an electric mixer, beat until well blended. Add eggs and vanilla and beat until smooth.

2. In a large mixing bowl, whisk together flour, baking powder and baking soda. Add flour mixture alternately with sour cream to the wet ingredients. Add chocolate chips and stir until blended.

3. In a small bowl, whisk together brown sugar, cocoa and cinnamon.

4. Pour half the batter into a Bundt pan that has been sprayed with cooking spray. Sprinkle half of the brown sugar mixture over top. Add remaining batter and top with the rest of the filling. Bake in preheated 350 degree oven for 40 minutes, or until cake tests done.

By Rona Cappell

Mum's Eggless Fruit Cake

Yield: 1 loaf.

1 cup sugar
3 tbsp. olive oil
¼ cup margarine
1¼ cups water
1 cup raisins
2 cups flour
2 tsp. baking powder
2 tsp. baking soda
½ tsp. cinnamon
½ tsp. nutmeg
½ tsp. ground cloves

Mum, the late Mrs. Ethel Abrahams of Landar, Cape Town and Jerusalem found this recipe in the Jerusalem Post in the 1970s and often made it for her grandchildren and guests.

1 In a saucepan, heat sugar, oil, margarine, water and raisins over medium heat. Bring to a boil. Cook until margarine has melted, stirring occasionally.

2 Whisk together flour, baking powder, baking soda, cinnamon, nutmeg and cloves. Pour hot ingredients into dry ingredients and mix thoroughly.

3 Pour into a greased and floured 9 x 5-inch loaf pan. Bake in preheated 325 degree oven until lightly browned, about 20 to 25 minutes. Cover loosely with aluminum foil and bake another 10 to 15 minutes, or until cake tests done.

By Rosalind Romen

NOTES:

Nut Sponge Cake

Yield: 12 servings.

Cake
6 eggs, separated
1 cup sugar
Pinch cream of tartar
1 tsp. vanilla
½ cup flour
1 tsp. baking powder
1 cup pecans, finely chopped

1 Place egg whites in mixing bowl of an electric mixer fitted with the wire whisk. Beat at medium-high speed until soft peaks form. Gradually add ½ cup of sugar and cream of tartar and continue to beat until stiff peaks form. Transfer to a large mixing bowl.

2 Place egg yolks in mixing bowl and beat on medium speed for 1 minute. Gradually add remaining ½ cup sugar and vanilla and continue to beat a few minutes longer.

3 In a small bowl whisk together flour and baking powder.

4 Fold egg whites gently into yolks. Carefully fold in flour and baking powder mixture. Fold in nuts.

5 Gently pour batter into an ungreased tube pan with a removable bottom. Bake for approximately 50 minutes, or until toothpick inserted in cake comes out clean. Invert pan and let cake hang until completely cooled.

SAUCE
1 cup whipping cream
1 cup dark brown sugar

In a small saucepan, whisk together cream and sugar over low heat. Cook sauce until thick, about 20 to 30 minutes. Invert cooled cake onto a serving plate. Pour 1 cup of the sauce over the cake. Drizzle the remaining sauce around the cake.

By Dolly Tarshis

Neapolitan Cake

Yield: 10 servings.

CAKE LAYERS
1 cup sugar
1 egg, lightly beaten
½ cup butter, softened
2½ cups pastry flour
⅛ tsp. baking soda

1 Place sugar and egg in a large mixing bowl and stir until blended. Add butter, flour and baking soda and mix on low speed with an electric hand mixer until combined.

2 Knead dough on a lightly floured surface until smooth. Divide into 3 equal parts. Line the bottom of three 9-inch layer cake pans with waxed or parchment paper. Press dough evenly into pans. Bake in preheated 350 degree oven for 18 to 20 minutes, until golden brown.

FILLING
1 large package chocolate pudding (6-serving size)
3 tbsp. chopped nuts

1 Cook pudding according to package directions, but use only 2 cups of milk to make the pudding thicker. Let cool.

2 Place one layer on a cake plate. Spread with ⅓ of the filling. Repeat with remaining layers, finishing with a layer of chocolate pudding. Sprinkle with chopped nuts.

3 Cover cake with a dome top and refrigerate overnight.

By Esther Mecklinger

NOTES:

Almond Crunch and Confetti Chiffon Cake

Yield: 12 to 15 servings.

ALMOND CRUNCH TOPPING
1 egg white
1¼ cups sliced almonds
2 tbsp. sugar

1 In a medium bowl, whisk egg white with a fork until foamy, about 30 seconds. Stir in nuts until evenly coated. Sprinkle sugar over top and stir.

2 Spread nuts in a single layer on a non-stick baking sheet. Bake in preheated 325 degree oven for 5 minutes. Stir with a wooden spoon to loosen nuts from baking sheet. Bake until golden, 5 to 8 minutes longer. Remove nuts from oven and stir once again to loosen them. Set aside.

CAKE:
1½ cups miniature semi-sweet chocolate chips
2¼ cups cake flour
1½ cups sugar
1 tsp. baking powder
½ tsp. salt
½ cup canola or corn oil
7 eggs, separated
⅔ cup water
1 tsp. vanilla extract
1 tsp. almond extract
2 tbsp. Amaretto liqueur
¼ tsp. cream of tartar

1 Place chocolate chips in the work bowl of a food processor and pulse until they become fine crumbs.

2 In a large bowl, sift together flour, 1 cup of the sugar, baking powder and salt. Make a well in the centre and pour in the oil, egg yolks, water, vanilla, almond extract and Amaretto. Using an electric mixture, beat mixture on medium speed until smooth and thick, about 3 minutes. Fold in chocolate chips and set aside.

3 Place egg whites and cream of tartar in a large mixing bowl. Beat on medium speed until foamy. Increase speed to high and beat until the movement of the beater forms lines in the mixture. Slowly add remaining ½ cup sugar, about 2 tbsp. at a time. Continue to beat until stiff peaks form.

4   With a large spatula, stir ⅓ of the egg whites into yolk mixture. Gently fold in remaining egg whites. Pour into an ungreased 10-inch tube pan with a removable bottom. Bake in preheated 325 degree oven for 1 hour and 15 minutes, or until cake feels firm to the touch. Invert pan onto a bottle with a narrow neck and cool thoroughly, about 1 hour. Carefully remove cake from pan.

GLAZE
1½ cups confectioners' sugar
3 to 4 tbsp. milk, soy milk, lemon or orange juice or water
½ tsp. almond extract

In a small bowl, whisk together ingredients for the glaze until smooth. Set aside 2 tbsp. of the glaze. Spoon the remaining glaze over the top of the cake, letting it drip down the sides and into the center hole. Cover the top of the cake with Almond Crunch Topping. Drizzle reserved glaze over top.

By Dr. Marvin Gelkopf

Pineapple Coffee Cake

Yield: 9 servings.

CRUST AND FILLING
1½ cups flour
½ cup butter or margarine, softened
1 14-oz. can crushed pineapple, well-drained

In a small bowl, blend together flour and butter until mixture resembles coarse oatmeal. Pat into the bottom of a greased 9 x 9-inch baking pan. Spread pineapple evenly over crust.

TOPPING
½ cup butter or margarine, melted
1 egg, well beaten
½ cup sugar
1 cup shredded coconut

In a small bowl, whisk together butter and egg. Add sugar and coconut and whisk until blended. Spread over pineapple. Bake in preheated 350 degree oven for 30 minutes.

By Leona Slotek

Skor Bar Cake

Yield: 10 to 12 servings.

6 Skor Bar chocolate bars, broken in small pieces
¾ cup brown sugar
½ cup sugar
½ cup butter or margarine, softened
2 cups flour
½ tsp. salt
1 egg
1 cup buttermilk
1 tsp. baking soda

1 Place Skor bars in the work bowl of a food processor fitted with the steel blade. Process for 10 to 15 seconds, until crushed. Transfer to a mixing bowl.

2 Place sugars and butter in the work bowl and process until blended, about 10 seconds. Gradually add flour and salt and process just until blended. Pour 1 cup of this mixture into the crushed Skor bars and set aside.

3 Add egg, buttermilk and baking soda to the remaining mixture and pulse with on/off turns, just until blended.

4 Pour half of batter into a 9-inch springform pan that has been sprayed with cooking spray. Top with half of Skor bar mixture. Add remaining batter, then top with remaining Skor bar mixture. Bake in preheated 350 degree oven for 1 hour.

By Lisa Draper

NOTES:

Plum Flan

Yield: 8 servings.

CRUST

1 cup flour

1 cup sugar

1 tsp. baking powder

¼ cup butter, cut in chunks

1 egg

1 tsp. vanilla

2 lbs. Italian prune plums, halved and pitted

1   Place flour, sugar, baking powder and butter in the work bowl of a food processor. Process for 10 to 15 seconds, until crumbly. While the machine is running, add egg and vanilla through the feed tube and continue to process another 10 seconds, until combined.

2   Press mixture into a 9-inch flan pan that has been sprayed with cooking spray. Arrange plum halves, skin-side up, on top. Bake in preheated 350 degree oven for 40 minutes.

CUSTARD

1 egg

1 tbsp. sugar

3 tbsp. melted butter

In a small bowl, whisk together ingredients for custard mixture until well blended. Pour custard over the plums and bake an additional 20 minutes.

By Elaine James

Brazilian Rocca Cake

Although this cake is small, it is very rich, so serve very small pieces. You can always serve a second portion!

Yield: 8 servings.

Cᴀᴋᴇ Lᴀʏᴇʀs

6 egg yolks

1 cup sugar

6 egg whites

2 cups ground Brazil nuts

1 Place egg yolks and sugar in a large mixing bowl. Using an electric mixer, beat until thick and lemon-coloured. Place egg whites in another mixing bowl. Beat until stiff peaks form. (Do not overbeat.) Gently fold into egg yolks. Carefully fold in nuts.

2 Pour batter into three 8-inch layer cake pans that have been buttered and lined with wax paper. Bake in preheated 350 degree oven for 30 minutes. Cool on racks.

Fɪʟʟɪɴɢ

½ pint (1 cup) whipping cream

2 tbsp. sugar

1½ tbsp. strong cold coffee

Sliced Brazil nuts and/or chocolate curls

1 Place whipping cream and sugar in a mixing bowl. Beat until stiff. Add coffee and beat a few seconds longer.

2 Spread whipped cream between cake layers and over the top. Decorate with Brazil nuts and/or chocolate curls.

By Ruth Richler

Nᴏᴛᴇs:

Fran's Favourite Chocolate Cake

Yield: 10 to 12 servings.

½ cup butter, softened
1½ cups sugar
2 egg yolks
½ cup cocoa
½ cup hot water
1 cup sour cream
1 tsp. vanilla
⅛ to ¼ tsp. peppermint extract (to taste)
2 egg whites
2 cups flour

1   Place butter and sugar in a mixing bowl. Using an electric mixer, beat until combined. Add egg yolks one at a time and beat until blended.

2   In another mixing bowl, whisk together cocoa and water until dissolved. Add sour cream, vanilla, peppermint extract and egg whites. Whisk until thoroughly blended.

3   Add flour alternately with cocoa mixture to butter/sugar mixture. Stir just until well combined. Pour into two 9-inch round cake pans lined with wax paper. Bake in preheated 350 degree oven for 25 minutes, or until cake tests done.

CHOCOLATE ICING
6 tbsp. butter, melted
4 squares bittersweet chocolate, melted
½ cup milk
2 eggs
½ tsp. vanilla
2 cups confectioners' sugar
¼ tsp. salt

1   In a small bowl, whisk together butter and chocolate. Set aside. Place milk, eggs and vanilla in another bowl. Using an electric mixer, beat on high speed for a few minutes, until well blended. Add sugar and salt and beat another 2 minutes. Add chocolate mixture and beat until well blended.

2   Place one cake layer on a cake plate. Spread with a layer of icing. Place second cake layer on top. Spread icing over top and sides of cake.

By Suzanne Schuchat

Rona Broman's Apple Cake

Yield: 12 to 15 servings.

2¾ cups flour
1¼ cups sugar
4 tsp. baking powder
4 eggs
1 cup oil
6 tbsp. orange juice
2 tsp. vanilla
8 apples, peeled and thinly sliced

1 In a large mixing bowl, whisk together flour, sugar and baking powder. In another large mixing bowl, whisk together eggs, oil, orange juice and vanilla.

2 Add dry ingredients to wet ingredients and stir just until blended. Fold in apples. Place in a 9 x 13-inch baking dish that has been sprayed with cooking spray. Bake in preheated 325 degree oven for 1 ¼ hours.

By Suzanne Shuchat

Mom's Apple Cake

Yield: 12 to 15 servings.

3 eggs, separated
1 cup sugar
¾ cup oil
1 tsp. vanilla
1¼ cups flour
2 tsp. baking powder
Pinch of salt
6 large apples, peeled, cored and sliced

1 Place egg whites in the bowl of an electric mixer fitted with the wire whisk. Beat on medium-high speed, until whites are stiff. Transfer to another mixing bowl and place in the refrigerator.

2 Place egg yolks and sugar in the bowl of a mixer fitted with the paddle. Beat on medium speed until blended. Add oil and vanilla and beat until blended.

3   In a large mixing bowl, combine flour, baking powder and salt with a wire whisk. With mixer on medium-low speed, gradually add dry ingredients to egg yolk mixture until combined. Fold in egg whites by hand.

4   Pour half the batter into a 9 x 13-inch baking dish that has been sprayed with cooking spray. Place apples over top. Cover with remaining batter. Bake in preheated 325 degree oven for 45 minutes to 1 hour, until golden brown.

By Renée Wolfe

Simple Apple Cake

Yield: 9 servings.

6 apples (preferably Spy), peeled and thinly sliced
½ tsp. cinnamon
1 cup flour
¾ cup sugar
1 tsp. baking soda
Pinch salt
½ cup oil
2 eggs, lightly beaten
½ tsp. vanilla

1   Place apple slices in the bottom of an 8 x 8-inch baking dish that has been sprayed with cooking spray. Sprinkle apples with cinnamon.

2   In a large bowl, whisk together flour, sugar, baking soda and salt. Add oil, eggs and vanilla and stir until well blended.

3   Pour batter over the apples. Bake in preheated 350 degree oven for 1 hour.

By Honey Sherman

Apple Custard Torte

Yield: 8 to 10 servings.

TORTE
¼ lb. butter, melted
1 cup sugar
2 eggs
1½ cups flour
2 tsp. baking powder
8 to 10 large apples, peeled, cored and sliced into eighths
1 tsp. cinnamon

1   Place butter in a large mixing bowl. Using an electric mixer, gradually beat in sugar until well blended. Add eggs one at a time, beating until well blended.

2   In another mixing bowl, whisk together flour and baking powder. Gradually add flour mixture to batter, mixing just until smooth. Spread evenly in a 9-inch springform pan that has been sprayed with cooking spray.

3   Stand the apple slices upright in the pan until the entire surface is covered. Sprinkle apples with cinnamon. Bake in preheated 350 degree oven for 1 hour.

CUSTARD
¼ lb. butter, softened
1 cup sugar
2 eggs

1   Place butter and sugar in a mixing bowl. Using an electric mixer, beat until blended. Add eggs and beat until thoroughly blended.

2   Pour custard over the top of the torte. Reduce oven temperature to 275 degrees and bake 20 to 25 minutes longer, until custard has set.

By Esther Mecklinger

Cinnamon Apple Cobbler

Yield: 10 servings

FILLING

¾ cup sugar

½ cup flour

6 to 6½ cups apples, thinly sliced

1 tbsp. sugar cinnamon

1   In a large mixing bowl whisk together sugar and flour. Add apples and stir until thoroughly blended. Sprinkle with sugar cinnamon.

2   Place mixture in a 7 x 11-inch baking dish that has been sprayed with cooking spray.

TOPPING

1½ cups quick-cooking rolled oats

¾ cups brown sugar

¼ cup flour

¼ cup butter, melted

1   In a large mixing bowl whisk together oats, brown sugar and flour until blended. Add butter and stir until blended.

2   Spoon topping evenly over apples. Bake in preheated 375 degree oven for 40 to 50 minutes.

By Rona Cappell

NOTES:

Lemon Swirled Cheesecake

Lemon curd is available commercially in gourmet shops or in the specialty section of many supermarkets, or make your own.

Yield: 16 servings.

CRUST
⅔ cup flour
2 tbsp. sugar
2 tbsp. chilled butter or margarine, cut into small pieces
1 tbsp. ice water

1 Place flour and sugar in the work bowl of a food processor. Pulse 2 or 3 times, until combined. Add chilled butter and pulse 6 times, or until mixture resembles coarse oatmeal. While processor is running, slowly pour ice water through the feed tube, processing just until dough forms a ball. Do not overprocess.

2 Firmly press mixture into the bottom of a 9-inch springform pan that has been sprayed with cooking spray. Bake in preheated 400 degree for 10 minutes. Cool on wire rack. Reduce oven temperature to 325 degrees.

FILLING
5 8-oz. packages light cream cheese, softened
1¾ cups sugar
3 tbsp. flour
2½ tsp. grated lemon rind
2 tsp. vanilla extract
¼ tsp. salt
5 eggs
1 cup Lemon Curd (e.g., Scotts)

1 Place cream cheese in a large mixing bowl. Using an electric mixer, beat at high speed until smooth. Add sugar, flour, lemon rind, vanilla and salt. Beat well. Add eggs one at a time, beating well after each addition.

2 Pour mixture into prepared crust. Spoon mounds of lemon curd over filling and swirl together, using the tip of a knife. Bake at 325 degrees for 1 hour and 15 minutes, or until cheesecake is almost set. Remove cheesecake from oven and cool at room temperature. Cover and chill for at least 8 hours before serving.

By Dr. Marvin Gelkopf

Cheesecake

Yield: 12 to 15 servings.

CRUST

35 single graham wafers, crushed

2 tbsp. melted butter

3 tbsp. sugar

⅛ tsp. cinnamon

In a small bowl, mix together all ingredients until well blended. Reserve about ½ cup of crumb mixture to use as a topping. Press remaining crumb mixture into the bottom and up the sides of a 9 or 10-inch springform pan that has been sprayed with cooking spray.

FILLING

6 eggs, separated

1½ cups sugar

2 lbs. creamed cottage cheese

1 pint (2 cups) sour cream

2 tbsp. cornstarch

2 tsp. vanilla

1 tsp. lemon juice

1   Place egg yolks and sugar in the mixing bowl of an electric mixer fitted with the paddle. Beat for 1 minute on medium speed. Gradually add cottage cheese and sour cream and beat about 3 minutes longer, until smooth and well blended.

2   Stir in cornstarch, vanilla and lemon juice and beat for 20 minutes. Pour mixture into a large mixing bowl.

3   Replace paddle with wire whisk. Place egg whites in a clean, dry mixing bowl and beat until whites are stiff, about 3 to 5 minutes. Do not overbeat. Gently fold into cheese mixture.

4   Pour mixture into crust-lined pan, filling it ¾ full. Sprinkle reserved crumb mixture over top.

5   Bake in preheated 325 degree oven for 10 minutes. Reduce heat to 225 degrees and bake 1 hour longer. Turn the heat off and leave cheesecake in the oven for at least 2 hours before serving.

By Denny Yolles

Crustless Sugar-Free Cheesecake

Yield: 16 to 18 servings.

1 lb. creamed cottage cheese
4 eggs
1 lb. cream cheese, softened
½ cup sugar (or Sugar Twin)
3 tbsp. cornstarch
3 tbsp. flour
1½ tsp. lemon juice
2 tsp. grated lemon rind
1 tsp. vanilla
½ cup melted butter
1 20-oz. container sour cream (2½ cups)

1 Place cottage cheese and 2 eggs in the mixing bowl of an electric mixer fitted with the paddle. Beat at medium speed until smooth. Add cream cheese and continue beating until smooth.

2 Gradually beat in sugar or sweetener and remaining 2 eggs. Reduce speed to low and add cornstarch, flour, lemon juice and rind.

3 Add vanilla, butter and sour cream. Beat until mixture is smooth.

4 Pour mixture into a 10 or 12-inch springform pan that has been sprayed with cooking spray. Bake in preheated 325 degree oven for 70 minutes. Turn off oven and let cheesecake cool in oven for 2 hours. Remove from oven and cool at room temperature for 2 hours. Refrigerate cheesecake for at least 3 hours before removing from pan. Garnish with fresh fruit (e.g., assorted berries) and chocolate shavings at serving time.

By May Cappell

Chocolate Cheesecake

Yield: 12 servings.

1½ cups chocolate wafer crumbs
¼ cup sugar
6 tbsp. butter or margarine, melted
¾ cup chocolate chips
2 egg whites
¼ cup sugar
1 lb. cream cheese
¼ cup sugar
2 egg yolks
1 large tub (16 oz.) Cool Whip

Garnish this cheese-cake with fresh fruit and/or chocolate shavings for a lovely presentation.

1   In a mixing bowl, combine chocolate crumbs, sugar and butter; mix well. Press into the bottom and up the sides of a 9-inch springform pan. Set aside.

2   Place chocolate chips in a microwavable bowl. Microwave on MEDIUM power for 2 to 3 minutes, or until melted, stirring 2 or 3 times. Let cool.

3   Place egg whites and ¼ cup sugar in a mixing bowl. Using an electric mixer, beat until stiff peaks form. Set aside.

4   Place cream cheese and ¼ cup sugar in a mixing bowl. Beat on low speed until blended. Add egg yolks and continue to beat until blended. Add melted chocolate and stir until blended. Fold in egg whites and Cool Whip.

5   Pour mixture on top of crust. Freeze several hours or overnight.

By Audrey Mallus

NOTES:

Cheese Pound Cake

Yield: 12 to 15 servings.

¾ cup butter, softened
½ lb. cream cheese, softened
2½ cups sugar
¼ tsp. salt
1 tsp. vanilla extract
1½ tsp. almond extract
6 eggs
3 cups cake flour

1 Place butter, cream cheese and sugar in a large mixing bowl. Using an electric mixer, beat until light and fluffy. Add salt, vanilla and almond extracts and beat until blended. Add eggs one at a time, beating well after each addition.

2 Stir in flour with a wooden spoon, mixing just until blended. Pour into a 10-inch tube pan that has been sprayed with cooking spray. Bake in preheated 325 degree oven for 1½ hours . Cool for 15 minutes. Invert onto a serving plate.

By Pamela Ramdeholl

Blueberry Crisp

You can make the topping in the food processor very quickly. Just combine all the topping ingredients in the processor and pulse several times, until combined.

Yield: 8 servings.

FILLING
6 cups blueberries
2 tbsp. brown sugar
1 tbsp. flour
1 tbsp. lemon juice

In a medium bowl, combine blueberries, brown sugar, flour and lemon juice. Spoon into a 7 x 11-inch baking dish that has been sprayed with cooking spray.

TOPPING

⅔ cup flour

½ cup brown sugar, packed

½ cup regular oats

¼ tsp. cinnamon

4½ tbsp. chilled butter or margarine, cut in small pieces.

1   In a large bowl, combine flour, brown sugar, oats and cinnamon. Cut in the butter with a pastry blender or 2 knives until the mixture resembles coarse oatmeal.

2   Sprinkle over the blueberry mixture. Bake in preheated 375 degree oven for 30 minutes until bubbly.

By Dr. Marvin Gelkopf

Easy Parve Apple Pie

Yield: 6 to 8 servings.

2 tbsp. flour

½ cup brown sugar

¼ tsp. cinnamon

5 cooking apples (Spartan or Empire), peeled and sliced into wedges

2 9-inch deep-dish frozen pie shells (parve), thawed

¼ cup brown sugar

½ cup flour

¼ cup cold parve margarine, cut into cubes

1   In a large bowl, whisk together 2 tbsp. flour, ½ cup brown sugar and cinnamon. Add apples and toss with flour mixture. Mound apple mixture into one of the thawed pie shells. (Do not remove pie shell from foil pan.)

2   In a medium bowl, whisk together ¼ cup brown sugar and ½ cup flour. Using 2 knives, cut in the margarine until mixture resembles coarse oatmeal. Sprinkle evenly over apples.

3   Invert the other pie crust over top of the apples and remove the top foil pan. Press edges of pie with a fork to seal. Cut several slits in the top crust so that steam can escape.

4   Bake on a cookie sheet in a preheated 425 degree oven for 10 minutes. Reduce heat to 350 degrees and bake until apples are tender, about 35 minutes longer.

By Cindy Berk

Key Lime Pie

Yield: 8 servings.

PIE CRUST
2 cups graham cracker crumbs
½ cup butter, softened
2 tbsp. sugar

1 Place all ingredients for pie crust in a mixing bowl. Mix together with a wooden spoon until well blended. Press mixture into the bottom and up the sides of a 9-inch pie plate that has been sprayed with cooking spray.

2 Bake in preheated 350 degree oven for 8 to 10 minutes, until lightly browned. Remove pan from oven. Reduce heat to 250 degrees.

FILLING
2 eggs
4 egg yolks
1 14-oz. can sweetened condensed milk
½ cup lime juice

1 Place filling ingredients in the mixing bowl of an electric mixer fitted with the paddle. (Alternatively, place ingredients in a large mixing bowl and use an electric hand mixer.) Beat on medium speed for about 5 minutes, or until well blended.

2 Pour mixture into baked pie shell. Bake at 250 degrees for 5 minutes. Remove pie from oven. Increase temperature to 350 degrees.

MERINGUE
4 egg whites
2 tbsp. icing or confectioner's sugar

1 While filling is baking, place egg whites in the mixing bowl of an electric mixer fitted with the wire whisk. Beat until soft peaks form. Gradually add sugar and beat until stiff peaks form.

2 With a spatula, spread meringue evenly over the hot filling. Bake for 3 to 5 minutes, or until golden brown. Chill before serving.

By Shanea Rakowski

Lemon Mousse Pie

Yield: 8 servings.

CRUST
⅓ cup butter, melted
1⅓ cups graham wafer crumbs
¼ cup sugar

Place melted butter in a mixing bowl. Add crumbs and sugar and stir until combined. Press into the bottom of a 9-inch pie plate. Bake in preheated 375 degree oven for 8 minutes. Let cool completely before filling.

FILLING
1 package lemon pie filling (Shirriff's)
3 egg whites
Lemon slices
2 tbsp. graham wafer crumbs

1 Prepare lemon pie filling as per package directions. Let cool completely.

2 Place egg whites in a mixing bowl. Using an electric mixer, beat whites until stiff peaks form. Gently fold egg whites into pie filling until blended.

3 Pour mixture into prepared pie crust. Garnish with lemon slices and crumbs. Allow to set in the refrigerator for at least 2 hours before serving.

By Rona Cappell

NOTES:

Coffee Ice Box Mousse

Yield: 15 servings.

¼ cup water
8 cups miniature marshmallows
3 tsp. instant coffee
2 cups crushed chocolate wafer crumbs
6 tbsp. butter or margarine, melted
9 or 10 chocolate wafers
4 cups (2 pints) whipping cream

1　In large saucepan, heat water over medium heat until boiling. Add marshmallows and coffee and stir until melted. Cool and refrigerate at least a half hour.

2　In a mixing bowl, combine chocolate crumbs and butter. Mix until blended. Press into the bottom of a 10-inch springform pan that has been sprayed with cooking spray. Line the sides of the pan with the chocolate wafers.

3　Pour whipping cream into a large pot (e.g., Dutch oven). With an electric mixer, beat cream until stiff. Fold in marshmallow mixture and stir until blended. Pour mixture into springform pan. Refrigerate at least 2 hours before serving.

By Suzanne Shuchat

Chocolate Orange Mousse

Yield: 8 servings.

3 egg yolks
¼ cup sugar
2 tbsp. orange liqueur
¾ cup semi-sweet chocolate, melted and cooled to room temperature
2 cups whipping cream

1.　Place egg yolks in the mixing bowl of an electric mixer fitted with the wire whisk. Beat at medium speed until foamy, about 3 minutes. Gradually fold in sugar. Add liqueur and melted chocolate and continue to beat 2 to 3 minutes longer, or until blended. Transfer mixture to a large bowl.

2 Pour whipping cream into the mixing bowl of the electric mixer fitted with the wire whisk. Beat on high speed until stiff peaks form. Gently fold into chocolate mixture. Pour into individual serving dishes. Chill before serving.

By Rona Cappell

Chocolate Trifle

Yield: 10 to 12 servings.

2 packages instant chocolate pudding (4 servings per package)
½ pint (1 cup) whipping cream
½ tsp. vanilla
2 to 3 tbsp. icing sugar
¾ tsp. instant coffee
1 store-bought sponge cake, cut in 1-inch chunks

Double this recipe if you are using a large trifle bowl. For extra colour and flavour, place a layer of raspberries between the pudding and the cake.

1 Prepare chocolate pudding according to package directions, but use 3¼ cups milk rather than the 4 cups that is specified.

2 Place whipping cream, vanilla and icing sugar in the bowl of an electric mixer. Beat on medium speed just until cream starts to thicken. Add instant coffee and ½ cup of the prepared pudding. Beat until stiff peaks form.

3 In a clear glass serving bowl, alternate layers of cake, pudding and whipped cream mixture, ending with whipped cream.

By Honey Sherman

NOTES:

Frozen Lemon Pie

This recipe works well for Passover using Passover mandlebroit for the crust. For an alternative crust, combine 1½ cups macaroon crumbs, ¼ cup melted butter or margarine and 2 tbsp. sugar. For an extra treat, serve with a raspberry coulis.

Yield: 12 to 15 servings.

CRUST

12 large mandlebroit, crushed into crumbs

¼ cup butter or margarine, melted

Combine crumbs and butter in a mixing bowl; mix well. Press into the bottom of a 9 or 10-inch springform pan that has been sprayed with cooking spray.

FILLING

6 whole eggs

6 eggs, separated

1 cup lemon juice

Zest of 1 lemon

2¼ cups sugar

6 tbsp. sugar

1   Place whole eggs, egg yolks, lemon juice, zest and 2¼ cups sugar in the top of a double boiler. Whisk together over medium-low heat until thick, about 3 to 5 minutes. Set aside to cool.

2   Meanwhile, place egg whites in the bowl of an electric mixer fitted with the wire whisk. Beat at medium speed about 2 minutes. Gradually add the remaining 6 tbsp. sugar and continue to beat until stiff peaks form.

3   Fold stiffly beaten whites into lemon mixture. Pour into springform pan. Freeze for at least 12 hours.

MERINGUE TOPPING

6 egg whites

5 tbsp. sugar

1   Place egg whites in the bowl of an electric mixer fitted with the wire whisk. Beat at medium speed for about 2 minutes. Gradually add sugar and continue to beat until stiff peaks form.

2   Cover frozen lemon pie with meringue. Broil for a few minutes, until golden brown.

3   Refreeze until ready to serve.

By Barbara Grossman

Frozen White Chocolate Mousse

Yield: 12 servings.

CRUST
2 cups chocolate wafer crumbs
¾ stick (6 tbsp.) butter, melted

1 Remove the bottom of a 10-inch springform pan. Butter the sides only. (If you butter the bottom of the pan, the crust will stick and it will be difficult to remove.) Insert the bottom back into the pan and set aside.

2 In a mixing bowl, mix together crumbs and butter. Press about ⅔ of the mixture onto the sides of the pan. Press the remaining crumbs onto the bottom.

3 Bake in preheated 350 degree oven for 7 to 8 minutes. Remove from oven and cool completely.

MOUSSE
12 oz. white chocolate
½ cup boiling water
4 eggs, separated
3 cups whipping cream
Pinch salt
⅛ tsp. cream of tartar
¾ cup sugar

1 Chocolate Mixture: Place chocolate in a large mixing bowl. Pour boiling water over chocolate. Whisk until smooth. Let stand for a few minutes to cool slightly. Add egg yolks one at a time, stirring with a wire whisk. Set aside and let cool completely.

2 Whipping Cream: Pour whipping cream into the large bowl of an electric mixer. Whip just until soft peaks form. Set aside.

3 Meringue: Place egg whites in another mixing bowl. Using an electric mixer, beat on high speed until foamy. Add salt and cream of tartar. Beat until whites hold a soft shape. Reduce speed to medium. Gradually add sugar, 1 tbsp. at a time. Increase speed to high and beat until meringue is firm, but not stiff and dry.

4 Carefully fold about ⅓ of the meringue into the chocolate mixture to lighten it. Gently fold in remaining meringue in two batches.

5 In a large mixing bowl, fold together the whipped cream and the chocolate mixture. Pour into the crust, smooth the top and place in the freezer for 1 hour. Wrap well and freeze for up to 2 weeks.

By Queenie Nayman

The best way to remove this mousse from the pan is to loosen the crust from the sides using a flexible spatula, then remove the sides of the pan. Next, loosen the bottom of the crust using a firm spatula. Transfer the mousse to a serving platter and garnish with dark or white chocolate curls. This can be done just before serving, or even a few days before.

Pretty Pie

*Fruit pies are
guaranteed crowd-
pleasers.*

This makes 2 balls of dough.

PIE CRUST

2 cups flour

1 tsp. sugar

½ tsp. cinnamon

½ tsp. salt

½ cup cold stick-type margarine or butter, cut in chunks

¼ cup cold vegetable shortening, cut in chunks

½ cup ice water

2 tbsp. graham cracker crumbs

1 egg white and 1 tsp. water

1 Place flour, sugar, cinnamon and salt in the work bowl of a food processor fitted with the steel blade. Process for 30 seconds. Add margarine and shortening. Process another 20 seconds, until mixture resembles coarse oatmeal. While processor is running, add water through the feed tube just until mixture gathers into a ball. Do not overprocess.

2 Divide dough in half. Cover and refrigerate dough while you make the filling.

3 Roll one ball of chilled dough on a lightly floured surface to form an 11-inch circle. Transfer to a 9-inch pie plate that has been lightly sprayed with cooking spray. Trim the dough to leave a 1-inch overhang. Sprinkle bottom of pie shell with graham cracker crumbs.

4 Spoon desired filling into the pie shell and cover with a Woven Lattice Top (see below) or a Plain Top (see below).

5 In a small bowl, whisk together egg white and water. Brush over top of pie.

6 Place the pie on a cookie sheet and bake in preheated 425 degree oven for 15 minutes. Reduce heat to 350 degrees and cook about 35 minutes longer, or until crust is golden brown.

WOVEN LATTICE TOP

1 Roll out the second ball of pastry into an 11-inch circle on a lightly floured surface. Using a pizza cutter, cut pastry into ten ½-inch strips. Weave into a lattice-top design as follows:

2 Keeping strips about 1 inch apart, arrange 5 strips crosswise over filling, letting the ends hang over the pie. Partially lift back the second and fourth strips. Place 1 strip lengthwise down the centre of the pie. Return the second and fourth strips back to their original position.

3 Working from the left hand side, partially lift back the first, third and fifth crosswise strips. Place a second lengthwise strip on the pie about 1 inch to the left of the length-wise centre strip. Return the first, third and fifth strips back to their original position.

4 Working from the right hand side, partially lift back the first, third and fifth strips. Place a third lengthwise strip about 1 inch to the right of the lengthwise centre strip. Return strips to their original position.

5 Working from the left hand side, partially lift back the second and fourth crosswise strips. Place a fourth lengthwise strip on the pie about 1 inch to the left of the second lengthwise strip. Return strips to their original position.

6 Working from the right hand side, partially lift back the second and fourth strips. Place a fifth lengthwise strip about 1 inch to the right of the third lengthwise strip. Return strips to the original position.

Plain Tops (3 Different Ways)

1 Roll ball of pastry into an 11-inch circle on a lightly floured surface. Gently lift the dough by folding it in half and lifting it with a large spatula. Place on top of filling. Neatly form the overhang into a decorative edge. Press your thumb all the way around the edge to form a fluted pattern. Cut a couple of slits in the top crust of the pie.

2 Roll ball of pastry into an 11-inch circle on a lightly floured surface. Using cookie cutters of different shapes (stars, hearts, etc.), cut out shapes from the dough. Place shapes on top of pie in an attractive design.

3 Omit the second ball of dough entirely. Do not trim the overhanging edges of the pie shell. Instead, fold it over to cover the outer portion of the filling, leaving the fruit in the middle exposed.

By Elise Mecklinger

Notes:

Red Raspberry Pie

Yield: 8 servings.

> 5 cups raspberries, rinsed and drained
> 1 cup sugar
> ¼ cup cornstarch or flour
> 2 tbsp. framboise liqueur
> 1 tsp. lemon juice
> 1 recipe for Pie Crust (pp. 216–17)
> 1 egg white and 1 tsp. water

1 In a large mixing bowl, gently combine raspberries, sugar and cornstarch with a wooden spoon. Add liqueur and lemon juice and stir until combined.

2 Spoon mixture into prepared pie shell. Cover filling with a Woven Lattice Top.

3 In a small bowl, whisk together egg white and water. Brush over top of pie.

4 Place the pie on a cookie sheet and bake in preheated 425 degree oven for 15 minutes. Reduce heat to 350 degrees and bake 35 minutes longer, until crust is golden brown.

Create Your Own Pie

Choose from a wide variety of berries (e.g., blueberries, strawberries) or combine different fruits (e.g., blueberries/ nectarines, strawberries/ rhubarb).

Yield: 8 servings.

> 5 cups sliced fruit
> 1 cup sugar
> ¼ cup cornstarch or flour
> 1 tsp. lemon juice
> ½ tsp. cinnamon
> 1 recipe Pie Crust (pp. 216–17)
> 1 egg white
> 1 tsp. water

1 In a large mixing bowl, combine fruit, sugar, cornstarch, lemon juice and cinnamon. Mix well. Place in prepared pie shell. Cover pie with a Woven Lattice Top (see above) or Plain Top (see above). Whisk together egg white and water. Brush over top of pie.

2 Place the pie on a cookie sheet and bake in preheated 425 degree oven for 15 minutes. Reduce heat to 350 degrees and bake 35 minutes longer, until crust is golden brown.

Almond Pear Caflouti

Yield: 8 servings.

4 firm ripe pears, peeled, cored and thinly sliced
2 tbsp. lemon juice
¾ cup all-purpose flour
½ cup plus 2 tbsp. sugar
¾ cup sliced blanched almonds
3 eggs, lightly beaten
½ cup unsalted butter, melted and cooled
½ tsp. vanilla extract
½ tsp. almond extract

1 Place pears in a mixing bowl and sprinkle with lemon juice. Set aside.

2 In a large mixing bowl, mix flour, sugar and almonds together with a wire whisk.

3 In another mixing bowl, blend eggs, butter, vanilla and almond extracts together with a fork.

4 Gradually add egg mixture to flour mixture and blend thoroughly with a wooden spoon. Stir in pears.

5 Pour batter into a 9-inch round cake pan that has been sprayed with cooking spray.

6 Bake in preheated 350 degree oven for 40 to 50 minutes, until lightly browned. Clafouti is done when a toothpick inserted into the centre comes out dry.

By Shanea Rakowski

NOTES:

Pavlova

Yield: 10 servings.

3 egg whites
½ tsp. salt
Pinch cream of tartar
3 tbsp. cold water
1 tsp. vanilla
1 tsp. white vinegar
1 cup sugar
1 tbsp. cornstarch
1 pint (2 cups) whipping cream
2 to 3 cups berries

1   Cover a large cookie sheet with foil. Outline a 9-inch circle on the foil and grease the inside of the circle.

2   Place egg whites, salt and cream of tartar in a mixing bowl. Using an electric mixer, beat on high speed until stiff peaks form. Add water, vanilla and vinegar and beat until blended.

3   In a small bowl, combine sugar and cornstarch. Add to egg white mixture 1 tbsp. at a time, beating well after each addition. Continue beating until thick and glossy.

4   Spread meringue mixture on the foil inside the circle to form a shell, piling it up slightly higher around the outside edges to make soft sides. Bake in preheated 275 degree oven for 1 hour. Turn off the heat and leave the meringue shell in the oven to cool.

5   To serve, peel off the foil and transfer the meringue shell to a serving plate. Beat whipping cream until stiff. Fill meringue shell with whipped cream and top with berries.

By Judy Hendler

NOTES:

Bienerstick Pastry

Yield: 8 servings.

DOUGH
1 cup flour less 3 tbsp.
3 tbsp. cornstarch
1 tbsp. sugar
½ tsp. baking powder
¼ cup butter or margarine, cut up
1 egg (add a little bit of milk if dough is not moist enough)

1   Place flour, cornstarch, sugar and baking powder in the work bowl of a food processor fitted with the steel blade. Process for a few seconds, until blended. Add butter and process until mixture is crumbly. While the machine is running, add egg through the feed tube and process a few more seconds, just until dough gathers into a ball. Do not overprocess.

2   Pat dough into the bottom and up the sides of a 9 or 10-inch flan pan that has been sprayed with cooking spray. Pierce dough in several places with a fork.

3   Bake in preheated 375 degree oven for 10 minutes.

TART FILLING
3 oz. butter or margarine
2 tbsp. milk
1 tsp. vanilla
4 tbsp. sugar
½ cup slivered almonds

1   In a small saucepan, heat butter over medium heat until melted. Gradually whisk in milk and vanilla until blended. Add sugar and whisk until blended. Stir in almonds.

2   Bring mixture to a boil. Reduce heat to low and cook 3 to 4 minutes longer.

3   Pour warm mixture into the cooled crust. It will be sticky, so work quickly. Bake in preheated 375 degree oven for 10 to 12 minutes. Cut into wedges while it is still warm.

By Judy Hendler

Make sure that this delicious tart is not overbaked. Be sure to cut it while it is warm because it turns crisp as it cools.

New Orleans Bread Pudding with Lemon Sauce and Whipped Cream

Yield: 6 servings.

PUDDING
3 large eggs
1¼ cups sugar
1½ tsp. vanilla
1¼ tsp. nutmeg
1¼ tsp. cinnamon
¼ cup unsalted butter, melted
2 cups milk
½ cup pecans, coarsely chopped
5 cups stale French or Italian bread cubes (leave the crusts on)

1   Place eggs in the large bowl of an electric mixer. Beat eggs on high speed until frothy and bubbles the size of pinheads have formed, about 3 minutes. Add sugar, vanilla, nutmeg, cinnamon and butter. Beat on high speed until well blended. Add milk and beat until blended. Stir in pecans.

2   Place the bread cubes in a greased 9 x 13-inch baking dish. Pour the egg mixture over top and mix together until the bread cubes are soaked. Let sit until you see a narrow bead of liquid around the pan's edges, about 45 minutes. Press the bread cubes down into the liquid occasionally.

3   Place pan in preheated 350 degree oven. Immediately reduce heat to 300 degrees and bake for 40 minutes. Increase heat to 425 degrees and bake until pudding is browned and puffy, about 15 to 20 minutes longer.

LEMON SAUCE
1 lemon, cut in half
½ cup water
¼ cup sugar
2 tsp. cornstarch
¼ cup water
1 tsp. vanilla

1   Squeeze 2 tbsp. lemon juice from the lemon halves into a saucepan. Heat over medium heat. Add lemon halves, water and sugar and bring to a boil.

2   In a small bowl, whisk together cornstarch and water. Stir into saucepan. Increase heat to high and cook 1 minute, stirring constantly. Strain, squeezing the sauce from the lemon rinds. Serve warm.

> WHIPPED CREAM
> 1 cup whipping cream

Place whipped cream in the small bowl of an electric mixer. Beat on medium to high speed until soft peaks form.

To serve: Put about 1 ½ tbsp. of warm lemon sauce in each dessert dish. Spoon ½ cup hot bread pudding over top and garnish with whipped cream.

By Marla Hertzman

Nanny's Baked Rice Pudding

Yield: 4 servings.

⅓ cup Thai fragrant rice
2 cups 1% milk
3 eggs, lightly beaten
½ cup sugar
½ tsp. vanilla
⅓ cup raisins (optional)
Cinnamon

This is my version of my grandmother's rice pudding. She did not know from Thai rice, but I still remember how good her rice pudding tasted.

1   Cook rice according to package directions. Cool.

2   In a large mixing bowl, combine cooked rice with milk, eggs, sugar and vanilla. Add raisins, if desired. Mix with a spoon until combined. Pour mixture into a 1-quart baking dish that has been sprayed with cooking spray. Sprinkle with cinnamon. Place dish in a larger pan that has been filled with hot water. The water should come about ⅔ up the sides of the baking dish.

3   Bake in a preheated 350 degree oven for 50 to 60 minutes, or just until set. To test for doneness, insert a knife in the middle of the pudding. If the knife comes out clean, then the pudding is done. Serve warm or cold.

By Sandy Hausman

Tiramisu

Yield: 8 servings.

6 eggs, separated
6 tbsp. sugar
1 475-gram container mascarpone cheese
2 cups cold strong coffee or espresso
¼ cup Frangelico (almond liqueur)
2 packages ladyfingers
¼ cup cocoa

1   Place egg whites in the bowl of an electric mixer. Beat on medium speed until stiff but not dry, about 2 to 3 minutes. Transfer to a large bowl.

2   Place egg yolks and sugar in the mixing bowl of an electric mixer. Beat on medium speed until light and fluffy, about 2 to 3 minutes. Beat in mascarpone cheese.

3   Gently fold egg whites into egg yolk mixture and blend thoroughly.

4   In a separate bowl, combine coffee with liqueur. Dip some of the lady fingers quickly into the coffee mixture and arrange them in a single layer to cover the bottom of a 9-inch plate. Cover with a layer of the cheese mixture. Sprinkle with some cocoa.

5   Repeat the dipping and layering process until all the ladyfingers, cheese and cocoa are used up, ending with a layer of lady fingers. Sprinkle lightly with cocoa. Refrigerate at least 1 hour before serving.

By Rona Cappell

NOTES:

Peach Sundaes with Caramel Pecan Rum Sauce

Yield: 6 to 8 servings.

> 1 3-oz. package cream cheese, softened
> ⅓ cup heavy cream
> ⅓ cup water
> 1 cup sugar
> 2 tbsp. dark rum
> 1 cup pecans, toasted and coarsely chopped
> 6 to 8 scoops of vanilla ice cream
> 6 to 8 ripe peaches, sliced and tossed with 1 tsp. lemon juice

1 In a large mixing bowl, whisk together cream cheese and heavy cream until well blended. Set aside.

2 In a medium saucepan, heat water over medium heat. Add sugar and stir until dissolved. Continue to cook the mixture without stirring until it turns a deep golden colour (300 degrees F on a candy thermometer). This will take about 8 to 10 minutes.

3 Remove the pan from heat and carefully pour in the cream mixture. Whisk over low heat until mixture is smooth. Stir in rum and pecans. Cover and store the sauce in the refrigerator for 5 to 7 days. At serving time, reheat on low heat, stirring often.

4 To assemble the sundaes, place scoops of vanilla ice cream into sundae glasses and top with sliced peaches. Drizzle with warm sauce and serve immediately.

By Debra Verk

Almond Cream Sundaes with Fresh Fruit and Chocolate Sauce

To serve, place equal amounts of fruit in parfait glasses and top each one with 2 tbsp. of mascarpone cheese mixture. Drizzle generously with warm chocolate sauce and top with almond pralines.

Yield: 10 to 12 servings.

ALMOND PRALINES
2 tbsp. unsalted butter
2 tbsp. sugar
Pinch salt
½ cup sliced or slivered almonds

In a large skillet, heat butter over medium heat. Add sugar and salt and stir until blended. Add almonds and stir to coat evenly, about 3 minutes. Spread almonds on a large plate to cool. Pat almonds with a paper towel to remove excess butter.

FRUIT SALAD
3 medium Bartlett pears, cut in ½-inch cubes
3 large peaches, peeled and cut in ½-inch cubes
1 pint strawberries, hulled and cut in quarters
3 large black plums, cut in ½-inch cubes
1 tsp. lemon juice
2 tsp. sugar

Place fruit in a large mixing bowl. Sprinkle with lemon juice and sugar and mix gently. Cover and refrigerate up to 3 hours.

ALMOND MASCARPONE
1½ cups mascarpone cheese
1½ tbsp. icing sugar
½ tsp. almond extract
½ tsp. vanilla extract

In a medium bowl, combine ingredients for Almond Mascarpone and mix until blended. Cover and refrigerate for up to 3 hours.

CHOCOLATE SAUCE
½ lb. semi-sweet chocolate
¾ cup whipping cream
1 tbsp. Amaretto liqueur

In a double boiler, heat chocolate over medium-low heat until melted. Add whipping cream and Amaretto and stir until blended. If using immediately, cover to keep warm. If not, refrigerate until needed, then reheat gently over low heat.

By Debra Verk

Blueberry Cake

Yield: 12 to 15 servings.

3 cups blueberries
5 tbsp. sugar
2 tsp. lemon juice
3 cups all-purpose flour
1 cup sugar
3 tsp. baking powder
1 tsp. salt
⅓ cup oil
3 eggs
¾ cup orange juice
1 tbsp. vanilla

1 In a mixing bowl, mix together blueberries, sugar and lemon juice. Set aside.

2 In a large mixing bowl, whisk together flour, sugar, baking powder and salt. Make a well in the centre. Add oil, eggs, orange juice and vanilla. Beat batter with a spatula or wooden spoon until smooth and shiny.

3 Pour ⅓ of the batter into a 10-inch tube pan that has been sprayed with cooking spray. Add half the blueberries. Repeat with another layer of batter, then a layer of blueberries. Top with remaining batter.

4 Bake in preheated 375 degree oven for 60 to 70 minutes, or until cake tests done. If cake starts to brown too much, cover top loosely with tinfoil.

By Dr. Marvin Gelkopf

Royal Crown Danish Ring

This magnificent brunch dessert is fit for a King (or Queen). You can start this recipe the night before and refrigerate the dough overnight. Then complete the recipe in the morning. Start baking it shortly before your guests arrive so that it will be fresh from the oven. The aroma of this sweet yeast bread will be impossible to resist. Your guests will definitely be impressed!

Yield: 12 servings.

1 tsp. sugar
¼ cup warm water (105–115 degrees F)
1 package (1 tbsp.) active dry yeast
1 cup milk
½ cup butter, softened
½ cup sugar
1 tsp. salt
2 large eggs
4½ cups flour

TOPPING
1½ cups brown sugar
2 tsp. cinnamon
1 cup finely chopped walnuts or pecans
½ cup melted butter

1 Dissolve 1 tsp. sugar in warm water. Sprinkle yeast over top and let stand for 8 to 10 minutes, or until bubbles appear on top. Stir to dissolve.

2 Meanwhile, in a small saucepan, heat milk over medium-high heat until almost boiling. Let cool until lukewarm.

3 Place butter, sugar and salt in the large bowl of an electric mixer fitted with the paddle. Pour scalded milk over top. Beat on low speed until blended.

4 In a small bowl, beat eggs for 30 seconds. Add to milk/butter mixture and beat until blended.

5 Add 4 cups of the flour and the dissolved yeast to the batter. Beat for a total of 5 minutes, beginning at a low speed, then gradually increasing to medium speed.

6 Replace the paddle with the dough hook. Add the remaining ½ cup flour and blend for 30 seconds at low speed. Knead at medium-low speed for 7 to 10 minutes, or until dough appears smooth and elastic.

7 Place dough in a large greased bowl, turning dough over to grease the top. Cover bowl with plastic wrap, then with a dish towel. Place in a warm, draft-free area to rise for 1 hour before shaping it. (OR place dough in refrigerator for 6 to 8 hours or overnight. If dough has been refrigerated, let it sit undisturbed for 1 hour at room temperature before shaping.)

8 In a small bowl, prepare topping mixture by mixing brown sugar with cinnamon and nuts. Set aside.

9 Punch down dough very lightly on a floured surface. Roll out into a thick slab.

10 Cut off pieces of dough and roll into balls about the size of a golf ball. Roll each ball in melted butter, then in topping mixture. Place two rows of balls, touching each other, in the bottom of a well-greased 10-inch tube pan. The outside row of balls should be slightly larger than the inside row. Sprinkle some extra topping mixture over top.

11 Cover and set aside in a draft-free area. Let rise until double in bulk, about 1 hour.

12 Bake in preheated 375 degree oven for 25 to 30 minutes. Remove pan from oven. Place a serving plate (and doily) face-down on top of pan. Flip pan upside-down to invert the yeast bread onto the serving plate. Let pan remain on the yeast bread for 1 minute before removing. Carefully remove pan. Serve while still warm.

By Linda Waks

Perfect Tea Biscuits

Yield: 12 to 14 biscuits.

2 cups flour
4 tsp. baking powder
½ cup vegetable shortening
Pinch salt
⅔ cup milk

These are easy and delicious. They're perfect with butter and jam. My kids love them and can make them themselves.

1 Place flour, baking powder, shortening and salt in a large mixing bowl. Using a pastry blender, chop mixture until it resembles coarse oatmeal. Gradually add milk and stir with a wooden spoon until it is well blended and gathers together into a ball.

2 With the heel of your hand, flatten dough to ½-inch thickness. With a glass, cut out circles 2 inches in diameter. There should be 12 to 14 biscuits.

3 Place on an ungreased cookie sheet. Bake in preheated 425 degree oven for 12 to 15 minutes.

By Wendy Kert

Banana Chocolate Chelsea

*It doesn't get more
decadent than this.
Well, maybe it could
if you spread some
peanut butter on top!*

Yield: 18 buns.

CHELSEA DOUGH
1 tsp. sugar
¼ cup warm water (105 to 115 degrees F)
1 package (1 tbsp.) active dry yeast
½ cup 1% or 2% milk (or lukewarm water)
3 to 3½ cups flour
⅓ cup sugar
½ tsp. cinnamon
½ tsp. salt
¼ tsp. grated orange zest
½ cup cold butter or stick-type margarine, cut in chunks
2 eggs (or 1 whole egg and 2 egg whites)

FILLING (ENOUGH FOR 2 ROLLS)
2 cups mashed bananas (2 or 3 bananas)
1 cup chocolate chips
½ cup brown sugar
1 tbsp. cinnamon

GLAZE
1 cup frozen orange juice
2 tsp. sugar

1 Dough: In a small bowl, dissolve 1 tsp. sugar in warm water. Sprinkle yeast over the water. Let stand for 8 to 10 minutes, or until bubbles appear on top. Stir to dissolve.

2 Meanwhile, in a small saucepan, heat milk over medium-high heat until almost boiling. Let cool until lukewarm.

3 Place 3 cups of the flour, sugar, cinnamon, salt and orange zest in a large mixing bowl. Stir with a wooden spoon until well combined. Cut butter into the dry ingredients with a pastry blender or 2 knives until the mixture resembles coarse oatmeal.

4 Make a well in the centre of the ingredients. Pour the yeast, eggs and milk into the well. Mix with a wooden spoon until a smooth ball forms, adding the remaining ½ cup flour if necessary.

(Note: If using a food processor or an electric mixer, proof the yeast, heat the milk and then place the dry ingredients in the work bowl or mixing bowl. Process or blend for 15 seconds, using the steel blade for the food processor or the dough hook for the electric mixer. Add butter and process or blend for another 15 seconds, or until mixture is crumbly. Add yeast, eggs and milk and continue to process or blend until mixture forms a smooth ball.)

5   Turn dough onto a lightly floured surface. Put flour on your hands and knead the dough for 5 minutes, or until dough is shiny and elastic.

6   Place dough in a large greased bowl, turning dough over to grease the top. Cover with a tea towel and let rise until double in bulk, about 1½ hours.

7   Punch down dough. Cut dough in half.

8   To make filling, mix all ingredients together with a fork. Set aside.

9   On a floured surface, roll half the dough into a 9 x 12-inch rectangle. Spread half the filling evenly over the dough. Roll up jelly-roll style, sealing edge well.

10   Cut the roll into 9 pieces and place cut-side down in a 10 x 10-inch baking pan that has been sprayed with cooking spray. Repeat with remaining dough and filling.

11   Cover pans with a dish towel and let rise for about 1 hour.

12   Bake in preheated 350 degree oven for 20 to 25 minutes, or until golden.

13   Glaze: In a small saucepan, heat orange juice over medium heat until melted. Whisk sugar into juice and stir until dissolved.

14   Using a pastry brush, spread glaze over buns.

By Elise Mecklinger

NOTES:

A Word From Our Sponsors

Basil Pita Triangles with Hummus and Red Pepper

Yield: 40 wedges.

PITA TRIANGLES
3 tbsp. Gallo Olive Oil
1 tbsp. fresh basil, chopped
½ tsp. Kosher salt
5 whole-wheat pita pockets

Preheat oven to 450 degrees. In a mixing bowl, whisk together oil, basil and salt. Cut each pita into 8 wedges. Place in a single layer on baking sheets and bake 4 minutes on each side.

HUMMUS
1 15-oz. can Unico Chickpeas, drained
¼ cup lemon juice
½ cup tahini (sesame paste)
1 tbsp. olive oil
1 clove garlic, minced
½ tsp. ground cumin
¼ cup chopped fresh cilantro (reserve some sprigs for garnish)
Salt and pepper
2 or 3 Unico Roasted Peppers, for garnish

Combine all ingredients except roasted peppers in a food processor fitted with the steel blade. Process until creamy and smooth. Adjust seasonings. Spread hummus on pita triangles. Top with strips of roasted red peppers in a criss-cross design over the top. Garnish with cilantro.

By Unico Inc.

NOTES:

Linguine with Fresh Tomatoes and Garlic

Yield: 4 servings.

SAUCE

3 tbsp. Unico Extra-Virgin Olive Oil

2 cloves garlic, minced

2 tbsp. chopped fresh Italian parsley

2 19-oz. cans Unico Diced Tomatoes, drained

Salt and freshly ground black pepper

⅓ cup chicken broth, if needed

1 In a large saucepan, heat oil over medium heat. Add garlic and parsley and stir for about 30 seconds. Add tomatoes; season with salt and pepper. Reduce heat to medium-low. Cook uncovered for 10 to 15 minutes, stirring occasionally.

2 Put the sauce through a food mill or food processor until puréed.

3 Return the sauce to the pan and keep it warm while the pasta cooks. If the sauce is too thick, stir in some chicken broth.

LINGUINE

6 cups water

1 tbsp. salt

1 lb. Unico Linguine Pasta

1 In a large saucepan, bring water and salt to a boil over high heat. Add linguine and cook according to package directions.

2 Drain pasta and pour into a heated serving dish. Add sauce and mix well. Adjust seasonings to taste. Serve immediately.

By Unico Inc.

Pollo Alla Cacciatore

Yield: 4 to 6 servings.

4 lbs. chicken parts
½ cup flour
4 tbsp. Gallo Olive Oil
1 medium onion, chopped
2 cloves garlic, minced
1 green pepper, seeded, cored and thinly sliced
10 mushrooms, sliced
1 28-oz. can Unico Diced Tomatoes
½ cup white wine
¾ cup chicken stock
1 bay leaf, crumbled
Pinch dried basil
½ tbsp. salt
Pinch pepper

1 Dredge chicken pieces lightly in flour. In a large saucepan or Dutch oven, heat oil over medium heat. Working in batches, cook chicken pieces for 7 to 10 minutes, until golden brown on all sides. Add onion, garlic, green pepper and mushrooms to chicken and cook 3 minutes longer.

2 Add remaining ingredients and reduce heat to low. Cover and simmer gently for 30 to 45 minutes, or until chicken is tender. Adjust seasonings to taste. Serve immediately.

By Unico Inc.

NOTES:

Fettuccini con Pollo alle Fiorentina

This is one of those dishes with lots of ingredients, but the final results are worth it – a delicious mélange of fettuccine with chicken and spinach! Perfect with crusty garlic bread.

Yield: 4 to 6 servings.

1½ lbs. boneless chicken breasts, cut in ½ x 2-inch strips
Salt and pepper
2 tbsp. Italpasta Olive Oil
Boiling salted water
3 tbsp. Italpasta Extra-Virgin Olive Oil
1 medium onion, diced
4 cloves garlic, minced
2 cups mushrooms, sliced
3 bunches fresh spinach, washed, stems removed, coarsely cut
½ cup dry white wine
4 large plum tomatoes, peeled, seeded and diced
1 tsp. Italpasta Tomato Paste
1 tsp. sugar
½ tsp. salt
Pinch black pepper, freshly ground
1 tsp. dried oregano
1 tsp. dried rosemary
2 tbsp. fresh basil, chopped
1 tsp. chili peppers, crushed (more or less if desired)
1 lb. Italpasta Spinach Fettuccini
Additional fresh basil, for garnish

1   Season chicken strips with salt and pepper. Heat 2 tbsp. olive oil in a large skillet over medium heat. Brown chicken strips on both sides, using tongs or a spatula to turn them.

2   Remove chicken and place on paper towels to absorb excess oil. Discard remaining oil and put the skillet back on the stove.

3   Bring a large pot of lightly salted water to a boil to cook the pasta.

4   Heat 3 tbsp. olive oil in a large skillet on medium heat. Add onions and garlic. Sauté until onions begin to turn golden, being careful not to burn the garlic. Add mushrooms and continue to sauté a few minutes longer. Add spinach and cook 1 to 2 minutes longer, stirring often, just until spinach begins to wilt.

5   Return chicken strips to the skillet. Add wine, tomatoes, tomato paste, sugar, salt, pepper, oregano, rosemary, basil and chili peppers. Stir well with a wooden spoon. Increase heat and bring to a boil. Then reduce heat and let simmer uncovered for about

5 minutes, or until excess liquid has evaporated and chicken is cooked but still moist.

6 Meanwhile, cook the fettuccini in boiling water until al dente. Drain well and place on a serving dish or individual plates. Pour sauce over pasta and garnish with basil.

By Italpasta

Burgundy Beef Stew

Yield: 4 to 6 servings.

>   2 lbs. stewing beef, cut in 1-inch cubes
>   ¼ cup all-purpose flour
>   3 tbsp. vegetable oil
>   4 medium onions, coarsely chopped
>   4 cloves garlic, minced
>   ¼ tsp. black pepper
>   1 tsp. paprika
>   1 cup red wine
>   4 OXO Beef or Vegetable Bouillon Cubes
>   3 cups boiling water
>   2 cups baby carrots, peeled
>   ½ lb. mushrooms, cut in quarters

1 Coat beef with flour. In a Dutch oven, heat oil over medium-high heat. Working in batches, brown beef on all sides, adding more oil as needed. Transfer beef to a bowl.

2 In the fat remaining in the pot, cook the onions and garlic until tender. Stir in pepper, paprika and wine. Add bouillon cubes which have been dissolved in boiling water. Stir in beef along with juices that have accumulated in the bowl.

3 Bring to a boil, stirring frequently. Reduce heat, cover and simmer about 1½ hours, until beef is tender, stirring occasionally. Add a little more water if the stew becomes too thick. Stir in carrots and simmer, covered, 20 minutes longer. Stir in mushrooms and simmer 5 minutes longer.

By Unilever

Fireside Warmer

Yield: 4 servings.

1⅓ cups water
3 Red Rose Regular or Naturally Decaffeinated Tea Bags
1 cinnamon stick, broken
2 whole cloves
⅓ cup sugar
1⅓ cups cranberry juice cocktail
1 cup dry red wine
Oranges wedges, for garnish (optional)

1   In a medium saucepan, bring water to a boil. Add tea bags and spices. Cover and brew for 5 minutes.

2   Remove tea bags. Stir in sugar, cranberry juice cocktail and wine; heat through. Remove spices. If desired, garnish with orange wedges.

By Unilever

Fast and Easy Chili

This mild chili is a great weekday meal idea since it's ready to serve in less than 30 minutes. Add more or less chili powder to suit your taste. If desired, add 1 diced green or red pepper.

Yield: 4 to 6 servings.

1½ lbs. lean ground beef
1½ cups water
1 cup tomato sauce
1 envelope Lipton Onion Soup Mix (or Lipton Spicy Onion Soup Mix or Onion Mushroom Soup Mix)
1 tbsp. chili powder
1 19-oz. can red kidney beans, drained

1   In a 12-inch skillet, brown ground beef over medium-high heat. Drain well.

2   Stir in remaining ingredients and bring to a boil. Reduce heat, cover and simmer for 20 minutes, stirring occasionally. Delicious over hot cooked rice.

By Unilever

Breakfast Berry Muffins

Yield: 12 muffins.

2 cups all-purpose flour
½ cup sugar
1½ tsp. baking powder
½ tsp. baking soda
½ tsp. salt
1 egg
½ cup orange juice
1 to 2 tsp. grated orange peel
1 square (½ cup) Fleischmann's Margarine, melted
1 cup berries (coarsely chopped cranberries, blueberries or raspberries), fresh or
  frozen

1 Combine flour, sugar, baking powder, baking soda and salt in a mixing bowl. In a smaller
   bowl, beat egg with orange juice, orange peel and melted margarine until combined. Add
   orange juice mixture to dry ingredients. Stir to blend. Stir in berries just until mixed.

2 Spoon batter into greased muffin cups. Bake in preheated 400 degree oven for 19 to
   20 minutes, or until tops spring back when lightly touched.

By Unilever

NOTES:

Cinnamon Apple Cheese Squares

A deliciously rich and comforting dessert that no one will be able to resist.

Yield: 8 servings.

⅓ cup Fleischman's Margarine, melted
2 packages (250 grams) cream cheese, softened
⅔ cup granulated sugar
1 egg
1 tsp. vanilla
1 cup finely chopped apple (about 1 large)
½ cup raisins
⅓ cup brown sugar, packed
2 tsp. cinnamon
8 sheets frozen phyllo pastry, thawed

1 Lightly brush a 7 x 11-inch (2 litre) rectangular baking dish with a thin layer of melted margarine. Reserve remaining margarine.

2 In a medium bowl, combine cream cheese, sugar, egg, vanilla, apples and raisins.

3 In a small bowl, combine brown sugar and cinnamon.

4 Keep phyllo dough covered with a damp cloth to prevent it from drying out. Lay 2 sheets of phyllo in prepared pan so that the edges overhang on all 4 sides. Brush phyllo with margarine. Sprinkle with ⅓ of the brown sugar mixture. Spread ⅓ of cream cheese mixture over top. Fold the 4 overhanging edges of phyllo over the filling. Brush with margarine.

5 Repeat layers twice more, using 2 sheets of phyllo for each layer.

6 Fold remaining 2 phyllo sheets in half (widthwise) and place on top. Brush with margarine. Bake in preheated 375 degree oven for 35 to 40 minutes, until golden brown. Cool on rack.

7 Dust with icing sugar before serving. Serve warm.

By Unilever

Kellogg's Easy-to-Fix Crispix Mix

Yield: 7 cups.

> 5 cups Kellogg's Crispix Cereal
> 1 cup bite-sized crackers
> ¾ cup unblanched nuts, any variety
> 2 cups raisins (optional)
> 2 tbsp. vegetable oil
> 5 tsp. dry Ranch salad dressing mix (or your own favorite seasonings)

1 In a large bowl, combine cereal, crackers, nuts and raisins.

2 Drizzle oil over cereal mixture. Using 2 spatulas, gently toss until well coated.

3 Sprinkle seasoning mix over cereal and toss again until well coated. Store in an airtight container.

By Kellogg Canada

Kellogg's Corn Flakes Crispy Cheese-Topped Potatoes

Yield: 6 servings.

Once you've tried this, you'll never want to have ordinary potatoes again!

> 4 medium baking potatoes, scrubbed
> 2 tbsp. melted butter
> Salt to taste
> 1½ cups grated old Cheddar cheese
> 2 cups Kellogg's Corn Flakes Cereal, crushed to 1 cup crumbs
> Paprika

1 Slice potatoes ¼-inch thick. Toss in melted butter. Place slightly overlapping potato slices on a 15 x 10 x 3/4-inch baking sheet that has been lined with foil and greased. Sprinkle potatoes lightly with salt. Bake uncovered in preheated 375 degree oven for 15 minutes.

2 Remove potatoes from oven and sprinkle with cheese. Top with crushed cereal and sprinkle lightly with paprika. Return to oven and bake about 25 minutes longer, or until potatoes are tender.

By Kellogg Canada

Blueberry Bran Muffins

Moist, flavourful and fibre-rich, these appealing muffins contain less than 30% of calories from total fat.

Yield: 12 muffins.

½ cup all-purpose flour
½ cup whole wheat flour
2 tsp. baking powder
¼ tsp. baking soda
¼ tsp. salt
1¼ cups Kellogg's All-Bran Cereal
½ cup skim milk
½ cup orange juice
1 egg
3 tbsp. vegetable oil
½ cup brown sugar, firmly packed
1 cup blueberries, fresh or frozen, unthawed

1 Stir together flours, baking powder, soda and salt. Set aside.

2 In a large bowl, stir together All-Bran cereal, milk and orange juice. Let stand 3 minutes or until cereal softens. Add egg, oil and sugar. Beat well.

3 Add flour mixture, stirring until just combined. Fold in blueberries. Spoon batter evenly into lightly greased or paper-lined large muffin cups.

4 Bake in preheated 400 degree oven for 20 to 25 minutes, or until golden brown and tops of muffins spring back when lightly touched.

By Kellogg Canada

NOTES:

Classic Wheat Bran Muffins

Yield: 12 muffins.

1¼ cups all-purpose flour
1½ tsp. baking powder
½ tsp. baking soda
¼ tsp. salt
1½ cups Kellogg's All-Bran Cereal
1¼ cups milk
¼ cup vegetable oil
⅓ cup molasses
1 egg
½ cup raisins

If desired, add 1 tsp. cinnamon and ½ tsp. nutmeg to the flour.

1   In a mixing bowl, combine flour, baking powder, soda and salt. Set aside.

2   In a large bowl, combine All-Bran cereal and milk. Let stand about 5 minutes, until cereal is softened. Add oil, molasses and egg. Mix well. Stir in raisins.

3   Add flour mixture and stir just until combined. Divide batter evenly into 12 lightly greased or paper-lined large muffin pans.

4   Bake in preheated 400 degree oven for 20 to 22 minutes, or until firm to the touch.

By Kellogg Canada

Rice Krispies Divine Toffee Squares

Yield: 24 squares.

1 cup all-purpose flour
¾ cup Kellogg's Rice Krispies Cereal
¼ tsp. baking soda
Pinch salt
⅓ cup brown sugar, firmly packed
⅓ cup butter or margarine, melted
1 can (300 mL) sweetened condensed milk
½ cup butter or margarine
½ cup brown sugar, firmly packed
½ cup semi-sweet chocolate chips
1¼ cups Kellogg's Rice Krispies Cereal

1   In a mixing bowl, thoroughly combine first 6 ingredients. Press into a greased 2 litre (8-inch) square baking pan. Bake in preheated 350 degree oven for about 10 minutes, or until just staring to brown.

2   In a heavy saucepan, combine condensed milk, ½ cup butter and ½ cup brown sugar. Over medium-low heat, bring to a full boil. Boil for 5 minutes, stirring continuously. Remove caramel mixture from heat and pour over baked crust.

3   Melt chocolate chips over low heat. Stir in remaining cereal until well coated. Carefully spread over caramel layer. Chill several hours to set. Cut in squares.

By Kellogg Canada

Kellogg's Cornflakes Grasshopper Pie

Yield: 8 servings.

3 tbsp. butter
2 tbsp. granulated sugar
3 squares (3 ounces) semi-sweet chocolate
4 cups Kellogg's Corn Flakes Cereal, crushed to 1 cup crumbs
1 jar (200 grams) marshmallow cream
¼ cup crème de menthe liqueur
1½ cups whipping cream

The added advantage of this refreshing dessert is its "no-bake" preparation, especially during the summer. If desired, garnish with additional whipped cream and chocolate curls.

1 In a small saucepan combine butter, sugar and chocolate. Stir over low heat until chocolate is melted. Stir in crushed cereal; mix well. Press firmly into the bottom and up the sides of a buttered 9-inch pie plate. Refrigerate crust while preparing filling.

2 In a mixing bowl, beat marshmallow cream with liqueur on low speed until smooth. In another bowl, whip cream to soft peaks. Fold whipped cream into marshmallow mixture.

3 Pour into pie shell. Freeze until firm. Remove from freezer about 20 minutes before serving.

By Kellogg Canada

NOTES:

Marcy Abramsky
Annette Addison
Salmina Ahmed
Leah Aryeh
Toni Baille
Lil Balsky
Judy Barkin
Cindy Berk
Lesley Binstock Offman
Harriet Bomza
Jack Borenstein
Shari Borenstein
Marlene Borins
Barbara Bregman
Simone Bronfman
Noreen Brown
Lesley Campbell
Rona Cappell
May Cappell
Trudy Cappell
Helen Chapnick
Ida Clarfield
Sherry Coote
Renee Daiter
Lisa Draper
Judy Freedman
Linda Friedlich
Ruth Frisch
Marvin Gelkopf
Norene Gilletz
Marlene Goldbach
Debbie Goldstein

Ellen Goldstein
Heather Gotlieb
Cheryl Graff
Mimi Green
Mrs. J. A. Griss
Barbara Grossman
Cora Hahn
Sandy Hausman
Judy Hendler
Marla Hertzman
Elaine James
Barbara Kerbel
Ellin Kert
Wendy Kert
Dolly Kerzner
Miriam Kerzner
Anna Koffler
Jacquie Kolber
Harriette Laing
Carol Lavine
Eleanor Long
Audrey Mallus
Elise Mecklinger
Esther Mecklinger
Sylvia Naftolin
Queenie Nayman
Phyllis Pepper
Nonie Plener
Esterita Rajsky
Shanea Rakowski
Pamela Ramdeholl
Lorraine Resnick

Ruth Richler
Rosalind Romen
Hilde Ronson
Miriam Rose
Ruth Rosen
Rina Rosenberg
Fern Sadowski
Candy Schnier
Caryl Schwartz
Carol Seidman
Marla Shapiro
Honey Sherman
Libby Shiller
Suzanne Shuchat
Hinda Silber
Judy Slan
Leona Slotek
Fran Sonshine
Renee Stein
Dolly Tarshis
Ann Tobe
Debra Verk
Linda Waks
Sara Waxman
Pearl Weiss
Faith White
Renee Wolfe
Lise Wolfson
Liora Yakubowicz
Denny Yolles
Estelle Zaldin